The Corporate Sufi

The Corporate Sufi

by Azim Jamal

Also by Azim Jamal

Seven Steps to Lasting Happiness:
An Inspiring and Practical Guide to Sustained
Happiness

Journal for Lasting Happiness: Your Daily Fuel for
Success

The One-Minute Sufi

AUDIO CD – Seven Steps to Lasting Happiness

Praise for
Seven Steps to Lasting
Happiness

"*Seven Steps to Lasting Happiness* is both inspiring and practical. Everyone will benefit from it."

Deepak Chopra, author of
How to Know God* and *Grow Younger, Live Longer

"*Seven Steps* is a beautifully written book that is bound to make a difference and touch many lives."

**John Kehoe, author of *Practice of Happiness*
and the international best-seller *Mind Power***

"Azim's book is a navigational aid that aims to tell people where they need to go, how to get there, and how to stay on course during the voyage. Jamal presents his findings in snack-sized bites, acknowledging that time is a precious commodity for most people. He wants readers to be able to open his book anywhere and immediately find something useful and illuminating. Using short chapters, uncluttered prose, personal anecdotes, and bold-faced instructions, Jamal presents the magnificent seven steps."

Mary Nolan, *Hamilton Spectator*

"*Seven Steps* is an honest, practical, and inspiring book that touches the essence of living. A valuable guide for people seeking balance, harmony, and lasting happiness."

**Robin Sharma, best-selling author of *The Monk Who Sold His
Ferrari***

"Good advice for achieving lasting happiness."

"A guide book where you are shown how the 7 steps can take you to lasting happiness. I like the opening first step of knowing or discovering oneself and the final step of enjoying the ride and encouraging people to do everything in between with enthusiasm."

"This book is full of healthy food for your mind and your soul. And whenever I follow this advice, I'm a much happier person. That's why I'll keep this useful guide handy, and be a better person for referring to it regularly."

"*Seven Steps* is a refreshingly clear, compassionate, and user-friendly handbook by a consummate team player who walks his talk. Every page provides a tool, a jewel, and a blessing for the reader."

"More than a guide book, this is a profound and passionate testimony to the power of love and spiritual balance that can heal and transform our lives."

"I thoroughly enjoyed reading the book."

"*Seven Steps to Lasting Happiness* is a motivational guide for people who want to create a better destiny for themselves and live their lives to full potential. It stresses the importance and illustrates the essence of balancing professional excellence, family harmony, healthy living, and humanitarian service in life."

Amanda Schuldt, *Balanced Life*

"The book examines questions such as how we can navigate through life; how we can succeed while remaining true to our principles, ethics, and values; how we can reach our fullest potential and accomplish our mission in life; and how we can be happy with whatever we have. The book is full of practical examples and stories that incite self-exploration."

Faranaaz Alimohamed, *Canadian Ismaili*

"Azim Jamal has created a recipe for long-term happiness with 7 simple ingredients… a timely contribution as we enter the new millennium. As a parent and Montessori principal, I found his book an invaluable tool in the pursuit of personal, family, and career development."

Lee Ann Mulrooney, founder, directress, and principal of Westside Montessori School, Vancouver, BC, Canada

Cover design by Bluestone Press Inc.
Cover photo by June Swadron
Illustrations by Jeff Schramm
Printed by Ameritech Printers Inc., DBA Print 1
Edited by Sam Meisel
Typeset by Sharon Boglari
Printed in the United States of America
First edition: May 2002

**National Library of Canada
Cataloguing in Publication Data**

Jamal, Azim, 1955-

ISBN 0-9685367-3-5

1. Business—Leadership 2. Sufism. I. Title.
BP189.2.J35   2002   297.4'173   C2002-910574-9

I dedicate this book to my parents, Abdul and Shirin, who have been my mentors.

Acknowledgments

I want to thank my wife, Farzana, who has been a pillar of support while I have pursued my new career, as well as an important part of my project, giving invaluable feedback and insightful suggestions; my daughter, Sahar, for all her witty input and help with typing adjustments; my son, Tawfiq, for his love and energizing hugs when I felt tired; and my parents and brothers, Mehboob and Shaffin, for their unconditional support throughout the process of writing and completing this book.

I also thank Sam Meisel for editing the book at various stages of its progression; Sharon Boglari for the typeset and consulting; June Swadron for the cover photo; Bluestone Press for the cover design; Mohamed Manji for consulting on all aspects of publishing, printing, and business management; Patryce Kidd for proofreading; Kend Pattar and Alnasir Kassam, our business associates, for their support and good work while I have been busy with writing and speaking; Laura Fluter for doing a fine job with the publicity and the promotion of the book and my speaking engagements; Jeff Schramm for doing a super job on the illustrations in short timelines; Akber Ladha, who has already crossed the bridge of life, for introducing Sufism to me; Larry Kazdan for his critique throughout the writing of the book and for always being honest with me; Ameritech Printers Inc., DBA Print 1 from Dallas, Texas, for doing an excellent job with the printing; Jonathan Cruz for taking the photograph of the author; Salim Kheraj, Shahirose Premji, Kerry Jothen, Shaffin Jamal, Taj Kavi, Salim Premji, and Salima Bhanji for their detailed and insightful feedback; Khalil Shariff for framing an important part of the Introduction and providing feedback; my friend Aziz Shariff for sharing creative ideas on marketing the book;

my cousins Nimira Bapoo, Zahra Kanji, Asheef Jamal, and Altaz Jamal for always being there to help and to make suggestions; Ali Lakhani for challenging some of my premises and encouraging me to go deeper into Sufism; Dr. Ali Asani for his guidance and insightful input; and Nurdin Dhanani for providing valuable suggestions with respect to the Introduction.

Thanks also to the following people for their valuable feedback: Richard Perl, Harold Karro, Amin Karsan, Amin Jamal, Noordin Nanji, Aziz Bootwalla, Pyarali Jamal, Taj Kassam, Shamim Jamal, Hassan Jiwani, Malik Talib, Rosie Bata, Alnoor Moosa, Nash Ramji, Gulam Panjwani, Shiraz Ali, Afzal Mangalji, Alnoor Kassam, Karim Hirji, Laura Fluter, Farid Daya, Wallie Dayal, Nadir Jamal, Amin Mitha, Mike Abdulla, Kamrudin Rashid, Shiraz Fazal, Hanif and Shehnaz Chatur, Roshan Dossa, Parvin Rahemtulla, Mubarak Alidina, Nasir Virani, Azeem Lakhoo, Nishma Kanji, Sultan Nazerali, Salima Kassam, Leo Sarantopolous, Shair Baz Hakemy, Shahid Punjani, Zahra Efan, Sabina Badal, Taj Nooruddin, Alnoor Aziz, Altaf Hirji, Amir Baig, Alnasir Ramji, Imamudin Saifu, Karim Chagani and Mohamed Thawer. Finally, I thank Shila Sunderji, Noory Kanji, and Khatija Jesani for helping me with the typing.

Most of all, I thank God whose mercy and grace stood as a beacon every step of the journey.

Thank you all.

Table of Contents

A corporate Sufi meditating and
connecting to an inner world.

My Journey to the Corporate Sufi

Until recently, I was a senior partner in a professional accounting firm where I had spent twenty years of my professional life. I made a comfortable living, after having spent a good number of years working hard to acquire three professional accounting degrees.

During those twenty years I did voluntary work, primarily in the area of motivational and inspirational speaking. Every time I spoke in this capacity, I discovered I had boundless energy and lost track of time, even though I was not paid to speak. These engagements changed me. I learned so much about myself, about life, about purpose, and about others, that I would have paid to get a chance to speak!

In the early 1990s, a recurring thought gave me no respite: What if I were to do inspirational speaking for a living? This would mean doing something I really loved doing, something in which I was talented and could make a difference. Why not? What was to stop me?

Initially, a thousand and one reasons came rushing in—both from myself and from others—as to why this was such an impractical idea. What? Give up your profession and the three professional degrees that you had worked so hard to attain? For many aspiring individuals this would be their life's quest! Why was I considering giving up something so valuable? Dealing with these thoughts was overwhelming.

So here I was, at the threshold of a dream; I had to make a choice. Either I live a life that I really want to live, or I live a life that others want me to live, a life wherein I would not perform with joy and reach my full potential. I persisted in thinking that the circumstances were not right, that I could not abandon my responsibilities, and that I could not go into a venture many people described as risky, even irresponsible. Nevertheless, my inner voice responded. Yes, committing myself to writing and speaking professionally could be risky, but there are those who do very well.

In the times of Shakespeare or Rumi (the 12th century Sufi poet), writers usually did well and became successful after they *died!* Today, excellent writers and professional speakers can do well during their earthly passage. I pondered the shining examples of Deepak Chopra (who has written over twenty international best-sellers), the Brazilian author, Paulo Coelho (who has also sold millions of copies of his books), and Stephen Covey (who has sold several million copies of his books and is a sought-after professional speaker). Another voice intruded: Yes, but these are the very few among the thousands in the writing and speaking field. My inner voice responded: Why can't I be one of the few who make it? What is to stop me from going all the way?

I began to feel empowered and realized two things. First, I understood that it was up to me, not anyone else, to succeed. It was not the fact that I had two young children, nor was it the unpredictable writing market that would determine my fate. It was entirely up to me to make the choice. If I believed I could do it, then I would do it.

Second, I was conscious of the Sufi way of looking at things. The spiritual giant, Rumi, wrote, "To a frog that's never left his pond, the ocean seems like a gamble. Look what he's giving up: security, mastery of his world, recognition! The ocean frog just shakes his head. I can't explain where I live, but someday I'll take you there." A frog will never know the beauty of the ocean if he remains in the pond. If I wanted to live to my full potential, if I were committed to exploring my innate gifts, I would not be able to do so in the accounting field because I was not passionately in love with it. Though risky, speaking and writing were fields to which I could commit myself and give my heart and soul, enjoying every moment of it. The picture was getting clearer.

But how was I going to convince my spouse whose support I would most definitely need? How was I to convince my parents whose blessings I would need? How could I help my parents understand that, after all those years of education and their loving investment in me, I would not end up in a volatile and risky business that would drain me of money and time? How could I get my children on my side, cheering for me and being proud of their dad? These thoughts were daunting.

It seemed that each time I overcame one hurdle or negative thought, another took its place. The easy thing to do would be to forget about my dream and pretend I had never thought of "jumping in the ocean." Just stick to accounting, Azim. I justified this conclusion by assuring myself that I could always spend some time speaking in a voluntary capacity and remain in my accounting profession full time.

My inner voice asked: Is that the best you wish for yourself? If you were to die today, would you be happy with how you spent your life? Could you face God and say that you did what you promised God you would do? I remembered Rumi who said, "I have a duty to perform. Do anything else, do a number of things, occupy your time fully, and yet, if you do not do this task, all your time will have been wasted."

I knew deep down and without a doubt what my answer had to be. The rest was just the details. I knew then that I had to do what I had come here to do and that all of the years of preparation, including being a senior partner and president of an accounting corporation, were what I had needed to prepare myself for this new path. I decided that I would make the switch with the blessing and the support of my spouse, parents, and children. My family's support was essential for my success, as well as being a principle that I spoke about. I also decided that I would do well financially in my new career. My motivation was to provide for my family and to make a difference to less fortunate people in many parts of the world.

In my many years of travel all over the world, I had seen poverty and sadness. I had seen fourteen Afghan refugees in Karachi living in a room as small as my children's bedroom and surviving on a dollar a day. I had seen people working fourteen hours a day in the blazing sun, making about a dollar a day. I had met children who had lost their father in war and seen a parent shot in front of their eyes. There were many such people—too many. There are approximately 6 billion people in the world today of whom 1.5 billion do not have enough to eat, 1.5 billion do not have enough clean water to drink, and 1.2 billion are living on less than a dollar a day. These people do not need just philosophies; they need the basic necessities of food, clothing, and shelter. I realized that I had a responsibility to live to my full potential and to make a difference to the world in which I lived.

These thoughts fueled my efforts at working hard, overcoming hurdles, and meeting challenges. I got the support of my professional associates and gradually began withdrawing from my work in the accounting profession. I did this slowly to make sure the transition for my partner and staff was smooth and to allow me, financially, to begin to invest in my new profession.

I began writing my first book, *The Corporate Sufi*. Yes, the very book that you are reading—except that I didn't complete it until May 2002, almost ten years after I began writing it! I was halfway to completing the book when I found I could not tie together the concepts of the book. I was trained as an accountant—a numbers man—not as a writer. I was beginning to feel hopelessness and despair. I stopped writing for a while, pondering my decision. Eventually, I began to write again—this time on a new book, *The Exalted Destiny*. This second book is still not complete, but I hope to complete it one day. Having completed two-thirds of it, I got stuck, again. I stopped writing, and almost returned to my accounting profession.

It was in April 1998, on a long flight back to Vancouver from Sydney, Australia, that my best-selling book, *Seven Steps to Lasting Happiness,* was conceived. I finished this book and self-published it in July 1999.

Once the book was published, I felt great relief and joy. As a man, I can never experience giving birth to a child, but publishing my first book was for me like giving birth. I felt a load off my shoulders! It was a promise fulfilled!

Unexpectedly, the completion of the first book made me realize that writing a book was only a beginning. An entirely new kind of work—promotion and marketing— was to begin—activities that made writing the book seem easy!

Having self-published my book, I was unaware that bookstores would not speak directly to authors. I did not have a publisher or a distributor to ensure that my book reached the bookstores. I had to find a distribution company. I was fortunate to find Hushion House in October 1999.

I was doing well with book sales at my seminars and had an excellent sales rate where I spoke, but the books were still unavailable in the bookstores. I was scheduled to do a few keynote addresses on "Lifelong Learning—a Key to Success" in the United Kingdom in February 2000, when, just before my trip, I went to Chapters, a large bookstore chain in Canada, to see if my book had arrived. Quietly entering the store, I went to the computer, typed "Seven Steps," and saw seventy titles with "seven"—but no sign of my book. Then I pressed "Happiness" and again saw seventy titles without any sign of my book. Anxiously, I typed A-z-i-m J-a-m-a-l, but still no sign of any books by this author.

I realized that my books had still not hit the stores. I had not understood the lead-time that distributors need to get books to stores. This was a really low point on my journey. In 1999 I had spoken approximately 170 times all over the world (United Kingdom, France, Portugal, Australia, New Zealand, and many cities in Canada and the United States) to over 100,000 people; I had spent 10,000 hours on this project but still could not get my book into the bookstores. I was very discouraged and wondered if my friends had been right about the risks associated with this kind of venture. As these thoughts swirled in my mind, I noticed a book in the bookstore. I tried to ignore it, but my eyes kept being drawn to its cover—to the point that I could not ignore it.

I picked up the book and read the introduction, the gist of which was that the author had fought in the Second World War, returned home, and started working on his childhood dream of writing a great American novel. After collecting rejection slip after rejection slip from scores of publishers, he found himself going broke. He never sold so much as a single sentence of his work to anyone. His wife and child left him, and he resorted to drinking.

One cold day in November he was walking in Cleveland and passed a pawnshop. His last $30 in his pocket, he saw a revolver for sale for $29. He writes that he was so pathetic that he did not have the spine to go into the pawnshop to buy the gun with which to end his life. He continued walking and ended up in a library instead. He decided to stay there because it was free and warm inside. He ended up in the self-help section, reading one motivational book after another.

The next day he went back to the library and read some more. He kept returning, spending countless hours reading these books in order to find out who he was. He came across a book entitled *Success Through a Positive Mental Attitude* by the insurance genius and philanthropist W. Clement Stone (co-authored with Napoleon Hill) which he adored. He read it a few times and vowed to meet the author one day. He found out that W. Clement Stone was the president of a national company that had a branch in the city where he lived.

Presenting himself at the branch one day, he applied for a job as a salesperson and got the job. He began to do well in his sales job—thanks to the motivational reading he had done. This led to a promotion, requiring him to move to Chicago where he was to write sales promotion material for the company's staff in the field. A year later he saw a notice at the office with an application for a position as executive editor of W. Clement Stone's magazine, *Success Unlimited*. Being imbued with a very positive attitude, he boldly applied for the job, although he knew next to nothing about editing a magazine. After several interviews and spelling out in detail what he would do to improve the quality of the magazine and its circulation, he landed the job.

It was at this time that the author wrote his first book, dedicating it to W. Clement Stone. How many copies could this guy, who so recently was about to shoot himself, sell? One copy to himself, a few to his friends, and some complimentary copies to the library? Guess again. He has sold more than 30 million books, having written 18 books that were translated into 22 different languages! He also became the most widely read inspirational, self-help author in the world. The author's name was Og Mandino and his first book was *The Greatest Salesman in the World*.

The success of *The Greatest Salesman in the World* was not immediate. As an unknown writer, he struggled to promote his work. His break came when W. Clement Stone read his book. Stone had gone to London where his wife, Jessie, gave him Og Mandino's book to read. W. Clement

Stone sent him a cablegram stating, "Your book is the most inspiring book I have read since *Magnificent Obsession*. See me upon my return."

At that time W. Clement Stone called Og Mandino's publisher, Frederick Fell, and ordered 10,000 copies of his book, one for every salesperson, employee, and shareholder of his company. Subsequently, Rich Devos, the dynamic president of Amway Corporations, recommended the book to all his staff and members. Og Mandino has never looked back. He fulfilled his Irish mother's dream of becoming a great writer and his own wish to meet W. Clement Stone—not only meeting him, but also winning his admiration and support.

Why am I sharing this story with you? Just to tell you the message the Universe was giving me: Why am I complaining about not having my book in Chapters? While I have never reached the desperation level of being down to my last 30 bucks and wanting to shoot myself, clearly, if Og can do it, I can too! I picked myself up and shortly thereafter, had a great speaking tour in the United Kingdom with excellent book sales in London, Birmingham, Leicester, and Edinburgh.

In 2000 and 2001, I spoke approximately 300 times all over the world to over 200,000 people, as well as spending a month doing full-time volunteer work in Central Asia. I got a big break when, on July 13, 2001, Deepak Chopra endorsed my book, *Seven Steps to Lasting Happiness,* stating, "Azim Jamal's work is both inspiring and practical. Everyone will benefit from it." That gave my book—and me—a great boost. Today I am a full-time professional inspirational speaker and a national best-selling author, having touched more than a million people with my message.

The big question that remains is: Have I realized my dream?

From one perspective, the answer is absolutely not! We never quite arrive. Every time we reach "there" from "here," then "there" becomes "here" and we have another "there" to aim for. So, throughout our lives we aspire to reach new goals. From that perspective, we only really arrive when we die.

From another perspective, the answer is a resounding yes! I am doing what I love doing; I am really passionate about my work, losing track of time when I am engrossed in it. I am traveling around the world speaking frequently. I have the full support of my spouse, the blessings of my parents, and the cheering from my children. Moreover, I am making a difference every day to myself and to others. I am doing what I had promised to do when I was born. If I were to die today, I would have no regrets. In this sense, I have definitely arrived.

Corporate Sufi Principles Applied on My Journey

- ❧ Marry my work with my life mission.

- ❧ Know that I am an instrument taking from one hand and giving with another.

- ❧ Life is uncharted territory—I am comfortable with the unknown.

- ❧ I persevere and am patient—I can do it!

- ❧ I am willing to take risks in order to find the truth.

- ❧ I don't worry about conventional wisdom.

- ❧ I have my near and dear ones on my team.

- ❧ My destiny is the journey.

Introduction

The Historical and Traditional
Connections of Sufism

The word Sufi, according to some research, is derived from the Arabic word *soof*, literally "wool," which refers to the material from which the simple robes of the early Muslim mystics were made. It symbolizes humility, simplicity, and purity, which are important virtues on the Sufi path.

Although Sufism traditionally has its origin in Islam, it has influenced many thinkers and philosophers. The Sufis are at home in all religions. Idries Shah, in his book *The Sufis*, says "They have no sacred city, no monastic organization, no religious instruments. They even dislike being given any inclusive name which might force them into doctrinal conformity."

Martin Lings, in his book *What Is Sufism?*, explains that all mysticism is equally universal in the greater sense that it leads to the One Truth, just like the radii of a circle all reach the center no matter where they begin from the circle. Sufism has wide appeal because of its universal messages, and its mystical dimension resonates with other faiths. Sufism is thus a bridge between east and west.

Jalaludin Rumi, the 12th-century Sufi master, describes a Sufi in his poem:
"What is the solution, O Moslems: for I do not know myself. Neither Christian, Jew, Zoroastrian or Moslem am I;
I am not an easterner or a westerner, or of land or sea;
My place is placelessness; my sign is of no sign.
I have no body or life; for I am of the life of life.
I have put away duality; I have seen the two worlds as one.
I desire one, I know one, I see one, I call one."

Rumi is describing a stage where he has transcended all forms of spiritual realization—which is very different from a merely theoretical understanding of spirituality. We are all friends and fellow travelers in the journey of life. Ultimately we all become one with God. The final stage a Sufi reaches is oneness with God, which comes when the ego has disappeared. Rumi says, "The mother of all idols is your own ego."

Who Is a Sufi?

A Sufi is interested in the essence, not the form. He looks at what is inside, not outside. A human being has an outward appearance—how we look, the clothes we wear, the car we drive, the house we live in, and the money we have. To the Sufi they matter little. It is what is inside a person, his character and spirit, that interests the Sufi. To the Sufi, the exoteric, or outward forms of an individual are an illusion; the reality lies in that which is esoteric, the inner part. The Sufi can be a man or a woman, young or old, black or white, a professional or a homemaker. Labels do not matter to a Sufi.*

The Sufi is grounded in ethical principles. He knows that these principles connect him to his core. He knows that no matter how much change there is around him, the ethical principles are changeless. Principles provide an anchor for the Sufi. The quest of the Sufi is to listen to his conscience and to follow it in both good and trying times. The Sufi knows that he can never get lost if he follows the true or straight path.

The Sufi is a person of timelessness and placelessness, living in the world but not of the world. While he is a mystic, he is not a hermit living on a mountain somewhere. Rather, he lives a balanced life, avoiding excessive materialism and striving for spirituality at his core. A Sufi views his role in this life as that of an instrument or vessel through which he takes with one hand and gives with the other. He goes with the flow, living in the moment but without losing sight of his vision.

A Sufi lives in the moment and adapts to the changing world around him without compromising the essence of his beliefs. He is a child of the moment. There are different forms of expression in Sufism, but the essence remains intact. The engaging verses of Sufi giants Ibn Arabi and Rumi, the love ecstasies of the early Sufi mystic Rabiah, the towering voice of Nusrat Fateh Ali Khan, and the prayer dances of the whirling dervishes are all expressions of Sufism.

*To facilitate ease of reading, I have used the pronoun "he" to include both genders.

Sufism traces its origin to the mystical traditions of Islam. It is the living spirit of the Islamic tradition. Sufism is built on submission and faith. A Sufi is one who sets himself on the path of self-purification leading to enlightenment and union with God. He is a seeker in search of his true identity. He seeks the truth with love. Love is the Sufi way. Rabi'a, the Sufi saint, was one of the earliest Sufi women to introduce the idea of selfless love for God. She said, "Love is a sea with unseen shores—with no shores at all." For her, love was the foundation and was boundless.

My Interpretation of And Approach to Sufism

Sufism is a varied tradition with a long and inspiring history. Its practices and doctrines are richly layered, and understanding them in their depths is a lifetime's work. I cannot explore this tradition in its fullness here, nor is it my purpose. I am neither a scholar nor a historian. For me, the Sufi is a symbol for a stance toward life and a perspective about values that we can all learn from and use in our daily lives. Sufism represents an ideal of how we can all maintain a spiritual and ethical center while still pursuing our worldly goals. It is this ideal that I want to explore in this book.

The Sufi quotations in this book are mostly translated works from different languages. These quotes have been taken from some of the books listed in the bibliography at the end of this book. The focus is on the message rather than its origin. So if a message conveyed reflects Sufi thinking, I have included it as a Sufi message, irrespective of its origin.

A Definition of "Corporate"

The word "corporate" is normally associated with a business setting, but in my book I have used this term to convey much more. Here "corporate" is associated with someone who has worldly ambition—to be successful and to do well in this world, in the workplace and in society at large. This definition includes CEOs, executives, senior managers, team leaders, middle management, group facilitators, partners, professionals, and employees. It also includes leaders such as school principals, teachers, board members, and parents. It also includes corporations. Consequently, in this book "corporate" encompasses a broad constituency or group.

People in the corporate world often struggle with some of the following issues:

- Dealing with stress from multifaceted demands
- Balancing their professional, family, health, and spiritual commitments
- Thriving and excelling amid an environment of constant change
- Managing themselves and their time
- Satisfying shareholder needs and demands
- Finding and retaining top talent by creating a con-

17

ducive work environment, encouraging creativity, and providing a learning and growing environment

- Developing and nurturing interpersonal skills
- Dealing with information overload and how to be selective
- Remaining focused on the top priorities
- Career and personal satisfaction
- Managing cash flow and staying profitable
- Facing the competition

By using Sufi messages and parables, the above issues are addressed in the book.

Who Is a Corporate Sufi?

A corporate Sufi is a person who marries his work with his life mission and balances his work, family, social, and spiritual lives. He is a person who is ambitious and wants to do well in the worldly sense of climbing the corporate ladder, raising a family, and being materially successful— without compromising Sufi principles. This book guides a corporate person to marry his worldly aspirations with the Sufi way of living.

Why would one want to be a corporate Sufi? Ultimately, we want fulfillment and lasting happiness. We do not climb the corporate ladder just for the mere sake of it but because we believe that corporate success will give us inner happiness, contentment, and satisfaction.

If we are worth 50 billion dollars but, in the process of acquiring that wealth, lose our family, our health, and the connection to our spirit, we will not find fulfillment and lasting happiness. The money we have made cannot buy back these things.

We spend a third of our lives at work. It is important to work in order to pay for the necessities and the luxuries. After a point, however, the excess money is only useful if we are able to make a difference with our wealth to our loved ones and to those who are less fortunate than we are. The best way to achieve happiness is to give happiness.

If we are not happy at work, if our work is neither fulfilling nor nourishing to the soul, a third of our lives is consumed to some degree by unhappiness. By being a corporate Sufi we are able to fuse our life's mission with our corporate mission. Our work becomes a prayer, a way of connecting to our spirit. We are able to remain effective, work with integrity and focus, and be a source of inspiration to those around us.

Envision yourself working in a field that not only nourishes your soul but also allows you to make a positive difference to yourself and to others. You lose track of time while doing your "work." It is work at which you are talented and gifted. You work hard at it because you want to work hard, not because you have to. It is like Wayne Gretzky working hard at playing hockey or Whitney Houston working hard at singing or Lee Iacocca working hard at running his company. You love the challenges and hurdles that come your way. You are not afraid to take risks and to venture into uncharted territory because you believe in your work.

Using This Book

By citing Sufi poems and anecdotes, I illustrate how using Sufi principles in a corporate setting can bring fulfillment, enhancement, teamwork and profitability. Also covered are practical tips and Action Items on how to:

- balance work, family, and spiritual needs,
- use the Sufi faith in the unknown when navigating uncharted corporate territory,
- link the Sufi search for the essence to the search for the corporate soul,
- apply the Sufi approach to eliminating the ego in order to become a selfless corporate leader,
- reach the top of your corporate ladder without giving up your ethics, principles, and inner happiness, and
- apply the Sufi principles in your day-to-day corporate activities.

A key message of *The Corporate Sufi* is that it is not how much we read that matters, but rather what action we take from what we have learned. Change takes place through reflection and action. Consequently, this book is designed in such a way that you read a section, reflect deeply on the message, and apply it as soon as you can in your corporate life. Action helps internalize your learning. Knowing that you are going to put into action what you have discovered keeps you alert and focused.

Continue to implement what you learn in the coming days. Practice creates habit and momentum. If you do this regularly, you will notice a marked improvement in your corporate life, and gradually you will notice your work life becoming more and more connected to your spirit.

To get the best use of the book, first read the entire book quickly to get the sense of its contents. Then read a section each day, reflect deeply on it, and implement it in your corporate life. Gradually, you will get a feel of what it means to be a corporate Sufi. Be ready for a pleasant surprise!

Azim Jamal
Vancouver, British Columbia
May 2002

1

Finding Our Purpose

❦

Knowing the One Thing We Must Do

*Working With Purpose Is Like Spending a Night
With a Lover*

Keeping Our Eye on the Goal

Life Is a Great and Noble Calling

❦

Ask the following questions:

❧ Do I know my purpose in life? Do I know the purpose of my corporation? Am I finding meaning and fulfillment in my corporate work?

❧ Is my life purpose married to my corporate purpose?

❧ Do I have a simply written, energizing corporate vision and mission statement that I clearly and consistently articulate to my team at work? Have I involved my team in preparing the company vision and mission statement?

Knowing the One Thing We Must Do

You have a duty to perform. Do anything else, do a number of things, occupy your time fully, and yet, if you do not do this task, all your time will have been wasted.

❧ **Rumi**

Rumi implies that we were born to fulfill a particular purpose in our lives. In turn, we were blessed with a unique gift—the ability to accomplish that purpose. Just as a honeybee knows it is born to make honey and is blessed with the necessary traits to do so, so too are we.

This purpose is entrenched in us before we are born physically. However, when we entered the world, we were attracted to the "toys" of life. They dazzled and tempted us, and we gradually became lost in their illusion. We became comfortable with worldly temptations and forgot our mission and purpose.

We spend our days and nights working hard to accomplish a million and one things, but we have to remember that if we do not perform the purpose we were born to carry out, our mission is incomplete. If we perform this one task, we have done it all.

We realize our potential when we work on our purpose. One way to identify that one thing we must do is to find an area of work that totally absorbs our attention when we are engaged in it. This is the area in which we can make a significant contribution. Reflect on the big questions of life: "Why am I here?" and "What will I leave behind when I'm gone?" These questions will prompt you to look deep within yourself to find that purpose for which you were born.

Our corporate purpose is an extension of our personal purpose. Dr. Stephen Covey uses the term "co-missioning," meaning the aligning of personal and company missions. It is integrating our work life with our soul to create a unified picture that brings together our inner and outer worlds.

If our life's purpose is not aligned with our corporate purpose, we experience tension and unhappiness. When the two are aligned, we find that we are performing optimally in our work life and are using our innate gifts.

If we do not work to fulfill that purpose, we will play the part an Indian poet thus describes, "The song I came to sing is left unsung. I spent my life stringing and unstringing my instrument." When we are singing our song, we become alive and are motivated and energized. Our work brings meaning and fulfillment. It is a wonderful feeling.

Working With Purpose Is Like Spending a Night With a Lover

There is a difference between spending a night with a lover and a night with a toothache.

❧ Sufi Saying

When we spend time with purpose, it is much like spending time with a lover—we are passionate and excited. We are driven and energized, upbeat, and positive. We do not worry about petty things. We lose track of time. On the other hand, when we work without purpose, it is like having a toothache. We experience pain and frustration. Lack of purpose can be a big impediment causing us to drift aimlessly through life.

We are enthusiastic when we do purposeful work. The word "enthusiasm" comes from the Greek word "enthous," which means inspired (in spirit). Purpose brings connection to spirit.

If we are sprinting to work, we are probably working with purpose. Our excitement and enthusiasm make our light shine from within, and we make a difference. Picasso said that it is our work in life that is the ultimate seduction. On the other hand, if we are crawling to work, it is time to step away from the rituals and get into reflection. We need to reflect on what kind of work will give us the highest satisfaction and enjoyment.

Mark Twain said, "The higher the pay in enjoyment the worker gets out of (his labors), the higher shall be his pay in money also." He called it "The Law of Work."

If our work is not fulfilling our purpose in life, we must be prepared to make some changes in our work life. Perhaps we can create a different environment at our current place of work. Or, we may need to switch careers or jobs.

Darren Entwistle, CEO of Telus, Canada, said that if you have the following three things at work, work becomes utopia. First, you are learning and growing. Second, you are having fun and making a valuable contribution. And third, you are being recognized and rewarded. If you have two of these three things, stick it out; if you have only one, it may be time to make some changes.

Remember: We have a choice.

Keeping Our Eye on the Goal

Obstacles are what you see when you take your eye off your goals.

❧ Sufi Saying

The Sufis believe that we should put all our efforts and concentration on the goal and not be distracted by obstacles. By so doing we will produce the energy needed to achieve our personal and corporate goals. The clarity of the goals makes this possible.

During World War II, parachutes were being made by workers who found their job boring and monotonous. Every morning the workers were reminded that every stitch they made in the parachute was potentially a life-saving action. It made the employees realize how their work made a difference and saved lives. It brought meaning to their work.

When a mother bird leaves her nest in the morning, her goal is to return with food for her baby birds. All day she stays focused on collecting food and does not give up until she finds enough food. She is driven by the goal of providing for her babies.

Mary Kay Ash, who was America's dynamic entrepreneur, wrote her goals on her bathroom mirror at home. This way she would have to look at them every morning.

By staying focused on our vision and purpose, we are able to overcome obstacles. Remember: Obstacles are part of the journey of life. When we keep our eye on the goal, obstacles are not threats. In fact, they become opportunities to create breakthroughs. The energy will come from focusing on the vision, not on the obstacles. Every time one door closes, 21 other doors are opening. In life every setback presents opportunities. So, where are we going to keep our eyes? We need to keep them on the opportunities and on the doors that are opening.

In professional soccer, scoring a goal and winning the game is the objective. This requires getting past the opponent's defenders (obstacles). If we focus on the goal, we will find a way to get past the defenders. Such is the case with corporate life.

If we find that things are getting unmanageable, we can break our tasks into smaller pieces. Our goals can be semi-annually, quarterly, monthly, or weekly. We can even further break down our weekly goals into daily goals.

Life Is a Great and Noble Calling

Work is love made visible.

❧ **Kahlil Gibran, author of *The Prophet***

Sufis believe that our life is a precious gift. A good portion of this life is spent at work. Therefore, it is important to make our time at work noble and meaningful. As John D. Rockefeller said, "The man who starts out simply with the idea of getting rich won't succeed; we must have a larger ambition."

The ambition has to be larger than self and includes making a valuable contribution to the world we live in. This brings meaning to our work. Agakhan III affirms, "Life is a great and noble calling, not a mean and groveling thing to be shuffled through as best as we can but a lofty and exalted destiny." When we are able to bring meaning to the workplace, we create energy that taps into the universal energy.

The vision expresses the corporation's aspirations. The vision needs to be energizing—something that gets everyone excited and motivated. Jack Welch, the CEO of General Electric, uses the term s-t-r-e-t-c-h. He says if we do not have "stretch" goals, we will never know our capacity to perform. In the process of reaching for the stars and realizing our vision, we ensure that the corporation's mission is not compromised.

Our team's involvement is crucial to building a vision and a mission statement. Without their understanding and commitment, these statements can become frames on the walls with no apparent function.

So, the concepts we need to integrate into our work life are clarity, simplicity, consistency, involvement, integrity, stretching, alignment, and communication.

Action Items

❧ Develop your personal mission statement. If you were to pick one thing you must do in your personal life, what would you choose? If you do not already have one, develop a corporate mission statement. If you were to pick one thing you must do in your corporate life, what would you choose?

❧ Align your corporate mission with your personal mission.

❧ Create excitement and meaning in your current work. Discuss with your employer how to create a win-win scenario. If necessary, make a change that connects your work with your purpose.

❧ Keep stretching your goals. They will keep you energized and expand your potential. If you are working as part of a team or corporation, involve people in goal-setting exercises to engender understanding of the corporate mission.

2

Embracing a Principle-Centered Approach

❦

Having Firmly Grounded Principles

Trusting the Voice of Our Conscience

Justifying a Wrong Does Not Make It Right

Promoting Love and Respect

❦

Ask the following questions:

- What are the values and principles that drive my organization? Are these an extension of my mission and vision?

- Does my team have a clear understanding of these principles?

- Are love and respect a part of these values? What is the trust level within the corporation?

- Do I immediately weed out anyone violating the values and principles of my organization?

- As a leader, do I hear and adhere to the voice of my conscience? Are all my strategies of climbing the corporate ladder grounded in ethics and principles?

Having Firmly Grounded Principles

A tree that is freshly rooted can easily be plucked. A tree that is firmly grounded cannot be removed, even with a crane.

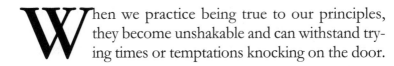 **Sa'adi, Persian Sufi poet**

When we practice being true to our principles, they become unshakable and can withstand trying times or temptations knocking on the door.

The Sufis believe that true and enduring success only comes with a strong foundation. The taller the edifice, the deeper and stronger the foundation. The same applies to our lives. Principles come before clients. They even come before family.

In sharing her mission, Katherine Graham, who was for a long time the only woman to run a Fortune 500 company, quoted one of her father's axioms: "In the pursuit of truth, the newspaper shall be prepared to make sacrifice of its material fortunes." She believed that the company's profitability was tied to this principle.

Henry David Thoreau wrote that a corporation "has no conscience, but a corporation of conscientious men is a corporation with a conscience." Therefore, the individuals who are part of the corporation reflect the corporation's principles.

Each corporate person has his own background and value system. The leadership should provide the right kind of modeling, training, and orientation that sensitizes everyone to the grave importance of keeping firm principles.

We can learn from the recent example of the international accounting firm of Arthur Anderson, which has federal criminal charges laid against it due to its role in the Enron Corporation case. In a related case, Enron Corporation, one of the Fortune 500 Companies, has filed for bankruptcy protection. If convicted of the criminal charges, the corporation will suffer dire consequences.

Ethical principles are the foundation for enduring success. Violations of these ethical principles can potentially tumble even the biggest corporations.

Trusting the Voice of Our Conscience

*As a splendid palace deserted by its
inmates looks like a ruin, so does a man
without character, all his material
belongings notwithstanding.*

❧ Mohandas Gandhi

Our conscience can help us live principle-centered
lives when we learn to listen to and to trust its
voice. The Sufis speak of a blind horseman who,
while riding a horse with his friend, drops his whip.
When he reaches down to pick it up, he mistakenly picks
up a snake instead. His friend implores him to throw
down the snake, but the blind man doubts his companion's integrity, thinking that he wants the better whip for
himself. This lack of trust cost the man his life, as the
snake bit him. When we trust the voice of our conscience
(our true friend), we are guided well.

In our lives, we will face many crossroads—the right path
may be long and full of obstacles while the wrong path
may be short and clear. If we choose the wrong path, we
will achieve success that is temporary and meaningless,
but if we opt for the right path, we will achieve fulfilling

and sustained success. We should always pay the price and follow the right path.

In a corporation, our conscience guides our mission statement and the values and principles emanate from the mission statement. As leaders, we get our guidance from this statement, and through self-awareness we remain true to our values.

In our corporate lives trust takes two forms. The first is the voice of each corporate person's conscience, and the second is the trust that we build within our team.

We work on eliminating rivalry that can lead team members to lose trust. If our team members are unhappy with their work, they may be tempted to violate their principles. A lot also depends on employee self-concept and self-esteem. When people feel good about themselves, they remain steadfast. As leaders, we can help by catching people doing things right, providing training, and keeping them happy and excited. With this encouragement, we keep the confidence of our team high and encourage them to stay true to their principles, no matter what.

Justifying a Wrong Does Not Make It Right

A man who was troubled swore that if his problems were solved, he would sell his house and give the profit to the poor. The time came when he realized that he must redeem his oath. But now he was reluctant to give away so much money, so he thought of a way out. He put his house up for sale for one piece of silver. Included in the deal, however, was a cat. The price tag for this cat was 10,000 pieces of silver. Someone bought the house and the cat. The man gave the single piece of silver to the poor and pocketed the ten thousand pieces of silver for himself. (Idries Shah in *The Tales of the Dervishes*)

In the preceding Sufi story the man strives to creatively justify a wrong, when in fact, he has not kept his word. In the final analysis, there is genuine loss of integrity, and, when he looks in the mirror, the man will find a tarnished reflection.

In breaking spiritual laws, the act itself becomes a punishment and sets into motion subtle forces whose consequences we cannot escape any more then we can escape the law of gravity.

In a corporate setting, when such a kind of creative violation takes place, the company loses its credibility, and this can have grave consequences. Missed sales targets can be dealt with, but violations of ethics and principles cannot. For this reason, we need to weed out the employees who violate the corporate integrity. Tom Peters, the well-known management consultant, says, "There is no such thing as a minor lapse of integrity." This is one thing that the corporation cannot compromise.

Leaders can encourage and promote training to enhance self-confidence, communication, and good relationships, stressing the importance of integrity.

A leader needs to send out a loud and clear message that the corporation has a zero tolerance for employees who violate the integrity of the corporation.

Promoting Love and Respect

Wind speaks not more sweetly to giant oaks than to the least of all blades of grass.

❧ **Kahlil Gibran**

I f nature is equally respectful to all creation, why do we humans discriminate? Whether it is the executive team or junior staff, respect is important.

Love is the Sufi way. Rumi says love can make beggars into kings and kings into beggars. Love transforms ordinary stones into rubies. Similarly it transforms people. When respect and love are present they get the best out of everyone including children.

At my son Tawfiq's school, the principal, Clive Austin, is a great example of someone who shows love and respect to the students. He knows almost everyone's first name and builds a bond with each one of the hundreds of children. This remarkable attitude brings out the best in the children.

In a corporation, the way we respect our staff will be the way they respect our customers. When we have a caring heart, people see that and perform better. They feel valued and cared for, and this builds trust.

We must remember that every person we meet in our lives is in some way our teacher from whom we can learn. Openness and humility are essential parts of promoting love and respect.

Our respect extends to the environment and having a social conscience. We conserve our natural resources, remembering that the earth has been given to us by our ancestors in trust and that we need to pass it on to our children. We belong to the earth—the earth does not belong to us.

Love and respect always win over hate and anger. Martin Luther King said, "We must meet hate with love. An eye for an eye leaves everyone blind." In a corporation, more gets done with love and respect than with bickering and strife.

Trust is the glue that holds relationships together. Trust is built from love and respect and is a cornerstone for our future success.

Love is a circle with no end. It has no boundaries. Ibn Arabi, the great Sufi Sheikh, says, "I proclaim the religion of Love, and wherever it carries me, this is my creed and my faith."

Action Items

❧ Ensure that the values incorporated in the mission and the vision are clearly understood and implemented. Train staff to deal with grey areas and have a process in place to deal with such issues.

❧ Apply zero tolerance for violations of ethics and principles.

❧ Create an environment at work that is founded on love and respect. Provide training to staff to improve self-concept, teamwork, and camaraderie. Respect all—staff, customers, and even competitors.

❧ Do one thing today that is right but difficult to implement.

❧ Encourage team members to assume personal accountability and to live the corporate principles.

3

Making a Difference

❧

Giving Creates Abundance

Corporate Success Is About Serving

❧

Ask the following questions:

❧ As a leader, do I allow creativity and imagination to flourish? Do I promote harmony and teamwork among staff?

❧ Is giving and serving very much part of my corporate life?

❧ Do I let people see how their actions make a difference?

Giving Creates Abundance

*For the bee the flower is the fountain of
life. To the flower the giving of pleasure
is a need and ecstasy. Be in your
pleasure like the flower to the bee.*

✿ Kahlil Gibran

The Sufis believe that giving is part of the law of
nature. All of Creation gives of itself in one way or
another. The cow needs to give of its milk to produce more, the sheep needs to be sheared to produce
more wool; the same applies to human beings who need
to give in order to achieve meaning and purpose in their
lives.

A candle loses none of its light when igniting another
flame. It is a win-win scenario. Rabi'a says, "I won't serve
God like a laborer expecting wages." Her life was about
unconditional serving founded on love. Such giving creates spiritual abundance.

In a corporate setting, drawing the best out of others is
emblematic of true leadership. A leader inspires people to
great heights by promoting harmony and teamwork,
believing in their abilities, noticing their efforts, and com-
mending them for their contributions. They elicit these
qualities by sharing their wisdom, guidance, and encour-

agement with the team. Through their acts of encouragement, leaders create abundance and catalyze peak per-
formances from their team. Leaders create a conducive
work environment through love and respect, breeding
creativity and providing learning and growing.

Through creating a stimulating corporate culture and
finding every opportunity to make a difference, corporate
executives are able to find and retain the top talent that is
crucial for corporate success.

Firoz Rasul, the CEO of Ballard Power Systems and a
corporate Sufi in my eyes, was awarded an honorary doc-
torate at Simon Fraser University, British Columbia. In
his convocation address he expounded on the value of
giving and said, "I believe that the success my company,
Ballard Power Systems, has enjoyed is primarily because
we have more givers than takers. The members of the
Ballard team give generously of their time, their energy,
and their knowledge for the success of their team members."

Tim Berners-Lee, rated by *Time* magazine as one of the
greatest minds of the century, invented the World Wide
Web. Instead of founding his own company and seeking
fortune, Berners-Lee has devoted his skills to keeping the
World Wide Web open, non-proprietary, and free. This
was his way of giving to society.

Others have taken the route of doing well in their business and sharing their wealth for good causes. One such
example is Ted Turner, the broadcasting mogul and

Atlanta Braves owner, who gave $1 billion to the United Nations, stipulating that the money was to be used for humanitarian causes. The death of his sister from lupus as a teenager and his father's subsequent suicide have kept Ted firmly grounded and shaped his profound empathy toward those who suffer.

Giving to such worthy causes creates abundance. We are motivated to continue to do well because our wealth is making a difference.

Corporate Success Is About Serving

The path is the service of others, not prayer beads and dervish robes.

❧ Sa'adi, Persian Sufi poet

The Sufis say that real faith lies not in holding beads but in serving humanity. Similarly, in a business it is not about rituals—it is about service.

We need to take attentive instructions from Nature. The tree serves us by bearing fruit that can be picked and eaten, the clouds serve when they open up and provide rain which is essential for the survival of crops and wild vegetation. The flower gives of its fragrance to everyone who walks by. Service is inherent in nature.

Sam Walton, founder of Wal-Mart, now the world's biggest company, started with a small group of five-and-dime stores in Arkansas in 1962. Today Wal-Mart has 4000 stores and has sales of $1 billion a day. Its success depends on good service and low prices. More than 1.2 million people learn to smile and say "How may I help you?" every time a customer comes within three meters of them. It's the ten-foot rule advocated by the founder.

Walton was strong on the importance of service and customer satisfaction in business. Brian Tracy, the management consultant expert, says, "In business, as in life, you are rewarded to the degree to which you serve others."

Service also means providing for the needs of the employees. It means creating a winning environment wherein team players do not feel fear or insecurity, which can really dampen the spirit. Service means encouraging staff to collaborate towards a common end as opposed to competing with each other. This ultimately leads to better service for the customer.

Ryuzaburo Kaku, Honorary Chairman of Canon, defines *kyosei* as a "spirit of cooperation" in which individuals and organizations work together for the common good. When practiced by corporations, it can become a powerful force for social, political, and economic transformation. Kaku adds that many companies around the world believe that they have a moral duty to respond to global problems such as third world poverty and the deterioration of the natural environment. But few have realized that their survival actually depends on their response. Global companies have no future if the earth has no future. By practicing *kyosei*, a positive difference can be made in the areas of poverty and the environment.

The United Nations has calculated that every human being could be given enough food, shelter, sanitation facilities, and education to live comfortably for no more than the money spent annually on golf, and only one-thirteenth of what is spent on cigarettes.

It is possible to serve even the poorest of the poor and still be a viable and profitable business. Muhammad Yunus, founder and Managing Director of Grameen Bank in Bangladesh, says, "Poverty is not created by poor people. It is produced by our failure to create institutions to support human capabilities." Grameen Bank lends US $35 million every month as a commercially profitable bank. More important, it saves borrowers' lives. About half the borrowers rise above the poverty line within a decade of its first loan.

When service is our motto, our success is fulfilling and sustainable.

The flower gives of its fragrance to
everyone who walks by.

Action Items

❧ Practice *kyosei* by promoting harmony, teamwork, and collaboration through love and respect. Be mindful that what matters is how much you care, not how much you know.

❧ Catch people doing things right.

❧ Be willing to give at every encounter and every opportunity.

❧ Create a giving and sharing environment among the team members.

4

Embracing Life-Long Learning

❧

Learning From All Places and At All Times

Looking Deeper to Gain Insight

❧

Ask the following questions:

- Do I create a learning culture in my business? Do I budget for training?

- Do I treat the intellect of my staff as my most valuable asset?

- Do I make available all information needed by employees to help them make decisions?

- Do I search for better ideas everyday and everywhere? Do I get input from employees, suppliers, and customers?

- Do I make life-long learning a mantra of my company? Do I provide for learning life skills, including interpersonal skills?

Learning From All Places and At All Times

We ought not to be ashamed of appreciating truth and of acquiring it wherever it comes from, even if it comes from races distant and nations different from us.

✤ Al Kindi, Iranian philosopher

Al Kindi encourages the acquisition of truth irrespective of its origin. Pluck the flowers of truth from wherever they come.

Learning is all about keeping an open mind. We can learn from every encounter and experience—from cradle to grave. Every person we meet has something to teach us if we are open to learn. The mind is like a parachute; it only works when it is open.

When we keep an open mind, we realize that the fact that people are different from us is a source of strength, for we can learn from them. They broaden our outlook and educate us in a deeper way. When we are open to learning, life is an open book. Hazrat Ali, the foremost Sufi said, "Knowledge is better than wealth. You have to look after wealth; knowledge looks after you."

In a corporate setting learning is earning. Bill Gates became the wealthiest person on earth not through an inheritance, but through brainpower. Learning is place-less, and it happens everywhere and at all times. If we learn only in schools, our learning is limited. Truly successful business people attribute a higher value to learning from experience. Learning through experience is what defines a person. We are the sum total of our entire past. We are made up of everything that has ever happened to us.

We can learn valuable information from our employees, suppliers, and customers by hearing their views. We can provide regular training to our staff and develop a reward system for those team players who demonstrate an eagerness to learn. Training should be provided in areas of goal setting and developing interpersonal skills, as well as time management.

We learn from Nature as well; in it lies immense wisdom. Sa'adi says, "The leaves of green trees, for the one who contemplates, are like pages of a book. Every page is like a book about the gnosis of the Creator." If we understand how a leaf comes into being and how it eventually withers and dies, we will understand a lot about life.

Great success comes when preparation meets opportunity. In a corporate scenario, opportunities do come, but, in order to take full advantage, we have to be prepared. Preparation happens through life-long learning.

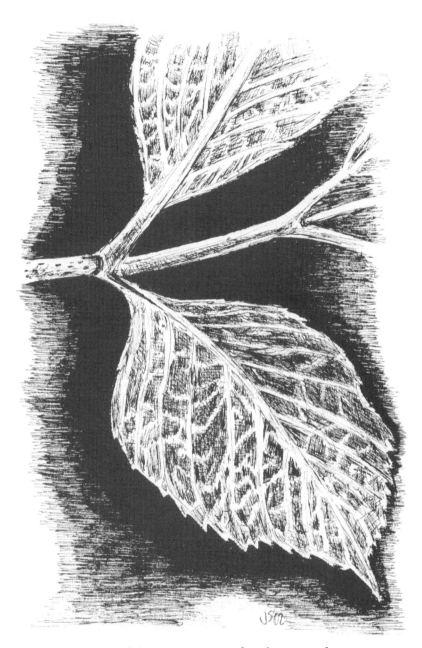

"The leaves of the green trees, for the one who contemplates, are like pages of a book. Every page is like a
book about the gnosis of the Creator." Sa'adi

Looking Deeper to Gain Insight

*Do not look at my outward shape, but
take what is in my hand.*

❦ Rumi

The materialistic environment attaches great value to physical and tangible things; it desensitizes us to matters of the heart and spirit. For the Sufi, matters of the heart and soul are far more important than physical and tangible things.

If we went by the uninviting outer shell of the coconut, we would never be able to taste the sweet water inside.

The Sufis go a step further and talk about learning with the inner eye. The inner eye is different from the naked or outward eye. We cannot see everything with our naked eyes. The air we breathe, the wind that blows, the love within, and the fragrance of a flower are all aspects that can be felt but not seen with the outward eye. The experience that occurs through the inner eye is a reality usually beyond description. It is often something we know for certain and can see and feel but is beyond description. As a traditional saying puts it, "The Sufis understand with the heart what the most learned scholars cannot understand with the head."

In a corporate setting, when we are able to transform data and knowledge into insight and wisdom, we can move far ahead of the crowd. This can be done with our intuitive faculties which are the workings of the inner eye and heart. John Wooden says, "It is what you learn after you know it all that counts."

In corporate life, being alert and seeing things from different vantage points are important skills. Not everything that appears on the surface is the same. Take the example of the honeybee and the bumblebee; they look alike, but from one comes honey, while from the other comes pain.

Action Items

❧ Invest in yourself; continuously upgrade your intellectual capacity.

❧ Instill the value of life-long learning within the corporation, and provide training and personal development for all staff.

❧ Develop a reward system to promote life-long learning, ensuring that all employees get better and better every day in every way.

❧ Schedule weekly meetings to discuss insights and to reflect upon what is working and what is not.

❧ Nurture an environment that develops the intuitive faculties of the team.

5

Having Faith in the Unknown

❧

Using Our Enormous Capacity

We Are Our Own Biggest Obstacles

Exploring Deep in the Sea

❧

Ask the following questions:

❧ Am I willing to risk all for my beliefs? Do I believe in myself or do I limit myself? Am I my own obstacle?

❧ Do I embrace change or do I fear it? Do I see change as a threat or an opportunity?

❧ Am I a trailblazer or a follower? Am I afraid to venture into uncharted territory?

❧ Can I live with a feeling of not knowing what I could have done had I tried?

Using Our Enormous Capacity

Look at your eyes; they are so small, but they can see enormous things.

❧ **Rumi**

The Sufis say, if we do not believe in ourselves, no one else will. Faith is a great virtue. We all have innate abilities and gifts, but, if we do not believe in them, they will not manifest themselves in our lives.

If we think small, we remain small. What the mind conceives, the mind achieves. If we go to the ocean with one bucket, we can get only one bucket of water. If we go to the ocean with one hundred buckets, the ocean gives us one hundred buckets of water.

The tiny silkworm produces the finest of silk, the honeybee makes the sweetest honey, and a tiny seed develops into a ripe and juicy fruit. We too are blessed with wondrous innate abilities.

Most of us do not use our full potential. We all have so much to offer. Some experts say that we use barely 10 per cent of our potential. Can you imagine the benefit to a corporation if this percentage were increased to 20 percent? Can you imagine the benefit to us as team players if we worked twice as effectively?

We have a glass ceiling—an imaginary boundary that we have created. We think of a little pool and stretch out to get as much as we can from this pool. Why, when we have a channel into the ocean, would we ask for water from a little pool? What stops us from living to our full potential?

There is no need to be afraid of uncharted territory. As Antonio Machalo says, "Travelers, there is no path. Paths are made by walking."

We Are Our Own Biggest Obstacles

You yourself are your own obstacle—rise above yourself.

❦ Hafiz, Persian Sufi poet

The Sufis say that you need to rise above your fears and apprehensions. They urge us to take risks and not to create imaginary barriers. We need to learn that failures are only stepping stones to our success. It is foolish to "blow on the yogurt if one was burned by the soup." One failure should not obscure our thinking over everything else.

Sufis encourage us to dare to venture into the unknown. If we don't push ourselves, how will we ever know our capabilities? Would the bird ever fly if it feared unbounded skies? Would we ever see a beautiful child if mothers were not courageous in facing the pain of childbirth?

In the corporate setting the more we fall, the stronger we become. The scars strengthen and tone our muscles, making us capable of facing bigger challenges. The greater the risk of failure, the greater the potential for success.

We ourselves are the biggest obstacles to all that we can be. There is no other real friend or enemy. When we take responsibility for our growth, happiness, and potential, the tide turns in our favor. We create the momentum, the "umph," the spark that ignites our innate power and wisdom. Remember: We can only show courage in the face of fear.

Stephen Covey says we must change the "want to" to "can do." If we want to make real progress, we need to find a cause that excites us, a cause we feel we can die for, a cause for which we can wager ourselves with confidence and dive in wholeheartedly. When we put a concerted effort into our cause without worrying too much about the risks and obstacles, we create unstoppable momentum.

The connection to universal knowledge is within us. Whatever we need to know is within us. All we need to do is to tune in to our inner self.

What stops us from living happily and making a difference? Who hampers our balance and harmony? It is none other than ourselves. The easiest way out is to assign blame to others: our spouse, children, boss, employees, customers, and so on. This gives us an escape from facing our inadequacies. The blame then lies somewhere else. Unfortunately, this kind of thinking also validates our helplessness in finding a solution. We convince ourselves we are not part of the problem. We will always find evidence to support our expectations. Beliefs shape our lives.

As aptly said by George Bernard Shaw, "Our lives are shaped not so much by our experiences as by our expectations."

Exploring Deep in the Sea

Deep in the sea are riches beyond compare, but, if you seek safety, it is on the shore.

✐ Sa'adi, Persian Sufi poet

T he Sufis are willing to assume risks in order to find the truth. They know that life is a mystery to live in and not to solve. The Sufis have faith in the unknown. They believe in the process of life and, above all, in God. They realize that only God knows everything, and they are comfortable with what they cannot always foresee. The Sufis, through their reflective and meditative nature, are connected with their spirit, and thus are in tune with their sixth sense.

When an astronaut begins his journey into outer space, he does not know what to expect but is rewarded with wondrous sights and discoveries. To know God we too must become comfortable with the unknown.

Similarly, in a corporate setting, worthwhile ventures entail dwelling in the unknown and having faith that they can be completed. Although we may feel the danger of losing everything, in reality we lose much by not diving in.

Thomas J. Watson, Jr., the founder of IBM, appropri-
ately said, "Lying dead in the water and doing nothing is
a comfortable alternative because it is without immediate
risk, but it is an absolutely fatal way to manage a business."

People who achieve greatness do so because they are
willing to take risks for a cause they believe in. Not to do
so surrounds them with a false sense of security that
takes them backward instead of forward. Safety and com-
fort zones are illusory securities that give us a false sense
of protection. As Helen Keller so aptly said, "Life is
either a daring adventure, or nothing."

Action Items

❧ Examine the root cause of your fears and actively attend to their eradication.

❧ Venture out and dare to do the things you thought you could never do—you will be amazed at what is possible.

❧ Believe in yourself—you are a marvel of creation.

❧ Wage your campaign totally, giving it all you've got.

❧ Trust and be comfortable with change and the unknown.

6

Persevering

❧

Giving It Everything We Have

Embracing the Struggle

❧

Ask the following questions:

- ✿ When the going gets tough do I give up and lose confidence?

- ✿ Do I learn from my falls?

- ✿ Do I yearn for instant gratification, or am I willing to be patient?

- ✿ Do I get easily discouraged by people around me? Am I surrounded by people who are positive and confident?

- ✿ How is the morale of my team at work?

Giving It Everything We Have

I lost everything I had, but in the process
I found myself.

❧ Rumi

Sometimes we may lose everything we have. We should not despair, but persevere and seek to find meaning in our loss. Even in losing everything, we can learn a few invaluable lessons. We learn the cycles of joy and pain, success and failure.

Kahlil Gibran says, "In every winter's heart lies a quivering spring, and behind the veil of each night waits a smiling dawn."

The spider is not daunted by the task of spinning its intricate web—it just goes ahead and does it.

In a corporate setting perseverance is a virtue that leads to fulfillment. When we embark on the journey to reach our goals, we must persist and persevere until we succeed. We cannot give up or lose faith. We have to hold on during times of pain and sorrow, for they are inevitable and will disappear if we can ride through them.

Perseverance goes hand in hand with patience; we may have to wait a while before we succeed.

A good example of a person who was both persevering and patient is that of Abraham Lincoln, who failed in business, lost his sweetheart, suffered a nervous breakdown, was defeated when he stood for election as Speaker, Senator, and Vice President, before eventually winning the U.S. presidential election in 1860.

Perseverance is an essential ingredient for success. It is the foundation on which great discoveries are made. This is true in most areas of endeavor, be it art, literature, or science. The struggle makes the victory even sweeter.

Ray Kroc, the founder of McDonald's fast-food chain, quotes in his autobiography *Grinding it Out,* "Press on: Nothing in the world can take the place of persistence. Talent will not; nothing is more common than unsuccessful individuals with talent. Genius will not; the world is full of educated derelicts. Persistence and determination alone are omnipotent."

At his convocation address to the graduates of The Institute of Technology in Madras, India, Azim Premji, the Chairman of Wipro, one of the largest high-tech corporations in India, said, "no matter what you decide in your life, you must persevere…" and he related the following touching story on perseverance.

An eight year-old girl learned that her brother was very sick and, since her parents were very poor, only a miracle would save the boy. She emptied her savings from a jar, the entire sum of one dollar and eleven cents, and went to the nearby store to purchase a miracle for her sick brother. The storekeeper was touched but replied that he did not sell miracles. A nearby customer overheard this conversation and said that he did sell miracles for precisely the amount of money the little girl had. The customer was Dr. Carlton Armstrong, a neurosurgeon, who went on to save the life of the little boy for no fee.

This story tells us that we can do anything we want to as long as we believe in our dreams and are willing to give it all we've got.

Embracing the Struggle

"Why are you doing this to me?"
*"So you can mix with spices and rice and
be the lovely vitality of a human being."*
*"Boil me some more...I can't do this by
myself."*

ᦥ Rumi

hen we realize how our strengths are deepened when we are tested, we begin to welcome those tests and challenges. Rumi gives an analogy of a chickpea that is being boiled for a meal. At first, the chickpea complains of pain and wants relief as soon as possible. When it comes to realize that through boiling it is going to become edible and be eaten by a human being, thus becoming part of a higher species and eventually attaining its destiny, it realizes that its freedom lies in the boiling. Understanding that the boiling leads to growth and eventual salvation, it says, "Boil me some more, I can't do this by myself."

Similarly, in our corporate lives we go through a kind of "boiling." A good example is that of Colonel Sanders, the founder of Kentucky Fried Chicken, who, at the age of 66, went bankrupt and had to go to 1009 restaurants to sell his recipe for fried chicken before someone agreed to buy it and give him 5 cents for every chicken sold. Yet

Colonel Sanders went on to became one of the most successful and respected businessmen in America. Most of us in a similar predicament would have given up after being rejected a few times. We need to learn from Colonel Sanders. As Winston Churchill used to say, "Never give in; never, never give in."

Rumi says that the grain is removed from the earth, resurrected in the ear of the wheat, and then threshed to become flour. The flour is kneaded and baked as bread. The bread is eaten by a person and becomes part of the human body and eventually part of human spirituality. Its development happens through struggle and dying of the old self.

How else can we appreciate the beauty of success if we have not felt the pangs of struggle? It is part of life; we cannot escape that. All we can do is to learn to thrive on it and to enjoy it. Instead of fighting pain, we befriend it, for in reality that is exactly what it is—a friend.

A youth once asked Thomas Watson, the founder of IBM, how he could succeed. Mr. Watson advised the youth to double his failures. The faster he failed, the closer he would be to succeeding. If there are a set number of times we are going to fail before succeeding, then we should get through these numbers quickly! In corporate life, if you have no struggles, you have no success!

Through pain, we tap into our innate abilities. It is this testing that triggers discoveries and breakthroughs in life.

Franklin Roosevelt was confined to a wheelchair as a result of polio, yet he was the only President of the United States of America to be elected four times. Beethoven was deaf when he composed some of his most enduring work. Professor Stephen Hawking was struck by amyothropic lateral sclerosis yet works with brilliance as a theoretical physicist.

These are but a few historical examples of men who embraced the struggle and achieved great results in spite of all of the difficulties. They showed that circumstances do not make you, they reveal you.

Action Items

❧ Do not be dismayed by obstacles and challenges.

❧ Never, never give up! Persevere until you succeed.

❧ Use your struggles to strengthen your resolve.

7

Being Effective Leaders

Drawing From the Inherent Strengths of People

Seeing the Full Picture

There Are Many Different Paths to the Same Truth

Ask the following questions:

- Am I an empowering leader who unleashes the full potential of my team? Do I remove all barriers that shackle my team?

- Am I raising the level of the game of my teammates? Do I lead by example?

- Do I promote cooperation and collaboration within my team? Am I in close touch with my teammates?

- Am I approachable? Do my teammates come to me with their challenges? Do I invest time in enhancing communication within my team?

- Does everyone in the company see the interconnected-ness of their work with others within the company?

- As a leader, do I allow the team players to use their individual strengths to accomplish corporate goals?

Drawing From the Inherent Strengths of People

No man can reveal to you aught but that which already lies half asleep in the dawning of your knowledge.

❧ **Kahlil Gibran**

The Sufis contend that true leadership is one that draws from the strengths of others. It is about awakening what is half asleep inside people. This requires that we inspire people to actualize their innate abilities.

In a corporate setting such leadership is very valuable. The ability to unleash people's potential, to energize them to use their talent and to work towards a common goal is a master skill of a true leader.

Some aspects of an effective leader that enables him to inspire and to ignite the potential of his team include:

❧ being a role model for his team

❧ being there as a coach

❧ empowering

❧ eliminating insecurities by trusting and believing in the inherent abilities and gifts of team members

❧ encouraging collaboration instead of competition
❧ involving the team in the preparation of a clear vision and mission
❧ giving sincere praise of team members at every opportunity
❧ showing empathy and caring
❧ rewarding excellence
❧ being result-oriented not task-oriented
❧ exhibiting clear, ongoing, and positive communication.

Effective leadership is all about people. You lead people from the right side of your brain, the more creative and intuitive side. You share your success with them, tap into their talents, and show them how their work makes a difference, so that their work becomes far more than just making a livelihood. You arouse their curiosity to learn more and stretch their imagination by encouraging them to aim high and to make decisions.

Leadership is about making leaders of your followers. People learn best when they have to teach others, so it is about unleashing the spirit of empowerment and involvement.

There is so much richness within each person to be discovered. Until it is discovered, it will forever be absent from the workplace. It is the role of effective leaders to nurture this richness.

Seeing the Full Picture

Rumi tells a story of a few blind people examining an elephant by sense of touch alone. Each person thinks that one part of the elephant is the whole and experiences it in a manner different from the others.

For one person, the elephant is a pillar (leg), for another it is a fan (ear), and for another it is a rope (tail). Yet they are all touching the same elephant. They may argue because their perceptions of what they are holding are different, but in reality they are touching the same elephant.

This Sufi story shows that we cannot look at things at the exclusion of the whole, for it will lead us astray and divert us from achieving our goals.

In a corporation, many different departments may handle various segments of the company's work. Tension, misunderstandings, and even turf wars may result if each department does its part without knowing the full picture. This can become counterproductive and affect the corporation's profitability. For the corporation to work in an integrated fashion it requires everyone in the company to have the full picture and an understanding of how one department's actions affect the entire company.

Another way of understanding this is to learn from the ants which, though they have different jobs, work to contribute to the whole picture by building the anthill and providing safety and shelter for the whole community of ants.

One has to look at the elephant as a whole, not just its
legs, trunk, ears or tail.

There Are Many Different Paths to the Same Truth

The ways to God are as many as the breaths of human beings.

❧ **Sufi Saying**

All creations of God have their own spiritual relationship with Him. The all-powerful God is not confined to any one religion or belief. God speaks through all religions, manifesting Himself in different ways appropriate to each seeker. There are many ways to get to the truth—but the truth is one. It is like many people climbing the same mountain along different paths.

Similarly, there are many different strategies that can be employed to realize the corporate vision, but the vision has to be the same.

People within a group have many different strengths. If we are leaders of a team or corporation, we tap into these different strengths. One way to do this is to allow people some flexibility of approach to their responsibilities—as long as they are getting the company to its goal. In other words, the approach is goal-based, as opposed to being strategy-based. If every team member were the same, there would be less creativity. The corporation must bank on the unique strengths of its team members. Sufis recognize the importance of diversity. It breeds strength, not weakness.

Lily Chiang, Executive Director of Chen Hsong Holding Ltd. in Hong Kong, ensures that her staff feel that they are contributing to the company's progress. She encourages her employees not just to come to her with problems, but to suggest solutions as well. If the suggestions are feasible, she lets them have it their way.

The effective leader plays the role of promoting unity in diversity, and ensures that everyone in the company feels useful and sees the full picture and interconnectedness of their work.

Action Items

❦ Raise the level of the game of all your team players. Get the best out of everyone by awakening what lies half asleep in them.

❦ Believe in the inherent gifts of people, remembering that everyone is gifted at something. Give them space to use their talents for the common good of the company.

❦ Always use the empowering model in your leadership. Decide with the team on the desired results, and be there for them if needed. Strive to make the corporation goal-driven rather than strategy-driven.

❦ Schedule regular meetings with your team in order to facilitate communication, reflection, assessment, and a platform to receive feedback. Stay away from finger-pointing and assigning blame. Be approachable by maintaining an open-door policy.

Ensure that everyone understands how their work affects the entire corporation.

8

Keeping a Positive Attitude

❧

Focusing on the White Cloth, Not the Dot

Using Our Mind Power

Being Content

Being Non-Judgmental

Letting Criticism Roll Off

❧

Ask the following questions:

❧ Do I worry about criticism?

❧ Do I keep an upbeat attitude when I hit bumps and hurdles along the way?

❧ Am I generally in good spirits, or am I constantly stressed and worried?

❧ Do I focus on the problem or the solution?

❧ Do I invest time in reflecting on my beliefs?

Focusing on the White Cloth, Not the Dot

When we see a big white cloth with a
dot, what do we see?

❦ Jalaludin Rumi

S ufis believe that each human being is innately good because he is created by God. He may have certain imperfections because he is human—only God is perfect. These imperfections need to be accommodated.

If we contemplate Nature, we understand that rainy days can be gloomy, though necessary to sustain plants and vegetation; sunny days are clear and bright, though they can make us hot and sticky and can dry up the vegetation. We need to focus on the good, making the most of it while accommodating what seems bad.

In a corporate setting, as in life, the tendency is to look at what is not working rather than at what is. This is problematic because the focus is on the problem instead of the solution. Focusing on the problem diverts our attention from finding a solution.

Rumi says that people focus on a small dot on a cloth and ignore the rest of the clean cloth. They look at problems in opportunities instead of looking at opportunities in problems.

When we look at the things that are working and encourage team players, we create positive energy. We get the best results when we utilize people's strengths. Tiger Woods concentrates on maximizing his strengths, as do many successful entrepreneurs and sports celebrities. When we work on our weaknesses, we can only make a little progress, whereas when we exploit our strengths, we amplify them.

Generally, we are good at certain things and not so good at others. Leadership can tap into this and try to encourage the team members to use their best talents in the interest of the team and the corporation.

It would be a waste for Sir Alex Ferguson, the soccer coach for Manchester United, to play David Beckham in defense when he is a great mid-field player and playmaker.

Using Our Mind Power

*You are your thought, Brother, the rest
of you is bones and fiber. If you think of
roses, you are a rose garden; if you think
of thorns, you are fuel for the furnace.*

✧ Rumi

You are what you think about all day. How can you be anything else? So, if you think good thoughts or invite good thoughts, that will determine who you become.

Sufis believe in the power of the mind or intellect. They believe that mankind is created as the crown of all creation. We have been blessed with intellect, which distinguishes us from all other creation. The proper use of intellect is the prime responsibility of every human being.

We are living in a meritocratic society, where more and more emphasis is given to merit and not to race, color, or social upbringing. We need to strive constantly to develop our skills. The human brain is more powerful than any existing computer; it has an immense capacity that is lying passive. Research says that we use a minute portion of our brain and that the rest remains untapped.

In a corporate setting, people who do well are those who have grand goals, planned strategies to achieve them, and positive expectations about the results. They invite the results by the creative energy they generate with their positive thinking and beliefs.

Throughout the day the corporate person meets challenges and problems. His thoughts determine his reaction and, ultimately, the outcome of these challenges. Every word we use affects our thinking. The use of the word "problem" is negative; use instead the word "challenge"—and the best word is "opportunity," which expresses optimism and the notion of a solution in the offing.

A wise person once said, "Be a star and light your own path. Do not worry about the darkness around you because that is when the star shines the brightest."

Be a star and light your own path, no matter how dark
it is around you.

Being Content

*Little but sufficient is better than
abundant but alluring.*

❧ Saying (Hadith) of Prophet Muhammed

The Sufis remain grateful for receiving all of God's bounty. They focus on the positive. The Sufis are not greedy; their ambition to do well is driven by the need to help others who are less fortunate. They value what is sufficient, not what is excessive.

Contentment is a prize enjoyed by fewer and fewer people today. Excessive materialism can cause much unhappiness. In the words of Gandhi, "There is always enough for the needy, but never for the greedy."

We can learn contentment from the tree that takes from the earth only as much water and nutrients as it needs, or from the earth which will not imbibe any more rain water than it needs, letting it sit on its surface until it is evaporated by the sun.

A corporate person's drive to make millions should be driven not by selfishness but with a view toward making a difference, helping one's family, aiding those who are less fortunate, and acquiring wealth through ethical means.

The attitude of gratitude and contentment creates a relaxed and confident demeanor. It portrays a person who is motivated and ambitious, yet unselfish. Colleagues feel comfortable around such a person, as he exhibits trust, respect, and friendship.

Being Non-Judgmental

*Out beyond ideas of wrong doing and
right doing, there is a field. I'll meet you
there.*

❧ Rumi

Sufis believe that judgments are made by human beings. God is not judgmental; He provides the means for us to learn from our errors so that we can grow and evolve.

We must realize that, although we have lived with ourselves for all our lives, we still grapple with knowing ourselves completely. How can we even begin to know or judge anyone else? Our judgments are only a reflection of our own paradigm and not an assessment of reality.

The Sufi's mind is like an umbrella, wide and open; it deflects others' flaws and weaknesses. He knows that everyone is playing his part in creation—big or small.

In a corporate setting we can take a non-judgmental attitude and give people the benefit of the doubt. By overlooking other people's shortcomings and realizing that everyone has faults, we make a positive difference in the lives of others.

Of course, we have performance standards and want employees to meet those standards. We do not want to be a nice guy who gets nothing done. We strive to be leaders who are clear about what we want to accomplish. Nevertheless, we endeavor to be gentle, helpful, and solution-oriented, thus providing the edge that gets things done, as opposed to someone who wastes energy and time by finger-pointing and assigning blame.

Assigning blame is a fruitless exercise that achieves little. It breeds discontent and alienation. It destroys the team spirit.

Letting Criticism Roll Off

No one throws a stone at a barren tree.

❧ **Sa'adi**

Criticism is normally thrown at people of substance, just as stones are thrown at trees full of fruit.

Sufis believe that, if we are driven from within and have sincerity of purpose, public opinion should not concern us. But, if we are unclear or have doubts regarding the sincerity of our actions, then we will be affected by criticism. We should be driven by sincerity of purpose without wasting energy on justifying and defending ourselves.

In a corporate setting, the only way not to be criticized is to do nothing—and even then you will be criticized! You are damned if you do and damned if you don't. The best thing is to do your best and leave the rest.

People who come up with ideas often get shot down with discouraging statements such as "It cannot be done," "It is a stupid idea," "It is too ambitious." Yet the ideas that are fresh and that challenge conventional wisdom are the ones that really create breakthroughs in society. So the next time your idea gets shot down, do not worry. Remember that no one throws a stone at a barren tree.

Criticism is no more than a personal opinion and stems from the paradigm of the person criticizing, and not necessarily from the reality of the situation. Shakespeare, one of the greatest poets of our time, was criticized by Lord Byron who said, "Shakespeare's name, you may depend on it, stands absurdly too high and will go down." Another example is that of the Duke of Edinburgh who is reported to have said of the Beatles, "The Beatles? They are on the wane."

Such criticism did not nullify the huge success of these artists.

Action Items

❧ Be solution-oriented, not problem-focused.

❧ Have confident expectations and think positive thoughts.

❧ Be non-judgmental and give people the benefit of the doubt. Always try to see the best side of people.

❧ Do not worry about criticism—just do your best and leave the rest.

❧ Do not expect perfection from your team.

9

Balancing Our Lives

✻

Balancing Our Lives

Seeing With Both Eyes

Focusing on the Important Matters

✻

Ask the following questions:

- What is my definition of real success?

- Am I balancing all my important roles in life? Do I enjoy holistic success and synergy of body, mind, and soul?

- Am I carrying my personal problems to work?

- Do I work with passion and reason?

- Do I waste time and energy on insignificant matters?

- Do I live with integrity so that 24 hours of my day are grounded in spirituality?

Balancing Our Lives

*A man should be in the marketplace
while still working with true reality.*

❧ **Sahl, Sufi mystic**

The Sufis believe in the balance between the physical world and the spiritual world. They encourage an integrated approach where everything they do is grounded in spirituality. They make spirituality the centerpiece around which everything revolves—everything they do from dawn to dusk.

Sufis consider the spirit and body to be one whole. They believe in integration, not dichotomies. What we do in our physical lives affects our spirituality, and vice versa. We cannot look at our lives in a vacuum. Our lives are integrated with our environment, ethics, and family. Sheikh Muzaffer says, "Keep your hands busy with your duties in this world, and your heart busy with God." Our faith has to be practiced daily within our corporate lives.

As the sun rises in the morning, a Sufi starts with a prayer and then works hard and ethically during the rest of the day. As the stars appear at the end of the day, he offers a prayer of thankfulness and tends to his family and health needs. A Sufi places much importance on his family . He ensures the home is full of love, affection and unity.

In the corporate world such an integrated life is very useful. A Toronto-based research team conducted a survey and discovered that 65 per cent of executives were overburdened with their workload which had adverse effects on the quality of their lives. This happens as a result of lack of balanced living.

Balance creates synergy. Synergy means creative cooperation leading to greater results. The better one part of our life is going, the more effectively it is able to support the other parts. The more the soul is nourished, the more it helps the body and mind. The healthier and more active the body is, the more it is able to help the soul and mind. The more the mind is positive and active, the more it helps the body and soul.

Mary Kay Ash said, "With God's help, every woman can find a way to bring balance in her life—no matter how great the obstacles." We need to pay more attention to our spiritual life and to rejuvenate it while we go about our material pursuits. This fusion brings about peace and harmony. As Novalis says, "The soul is where the inner and the outer world meet."

The most difficult challenge that most corporate people grapple with is balancing their corporate and personal lives.

When a corporate person's spirit, health, mind, family, and social needs are all met, he experiences holistic suc-

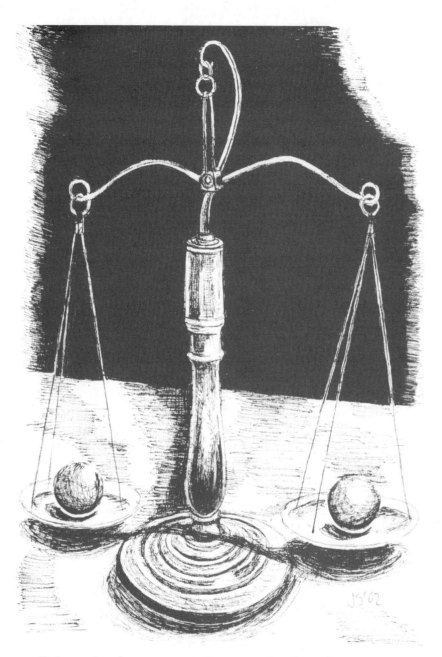

Balance is adequate attention to each of our important
areas of life.

cess that can be sustained over a long period of time. One of the ways to accomplish this is to wake up sixty minutes earlier in the morning than you do now and to use this time to do twenty minutes of meditation, twenty minutes of exercise, and twenty minutes of reading something inspirational. This will provide a headstart on the day. Make up for the lost sleep by going to bed an hour early.

Seeing With Both Eyes

*For reason, ruling alone, is a force
confining; and passion, unattended, is a
flame that burns to its own destruction.*

❧ Kahlil Gibran

The Sufis believe in the balance between reason and passion. The mind is rational and can transcend the emotions. But without passion, one cannot reach great heights. We need to take a balanced approach.

The intoxicated view is where passion takes over. The sober view is where reason takes over. There is merit in the marriage of the two. The Sufis believe that reason without passion is lame and that passion without reason is blind. Actions based on a balanced approach give us the best results.

In a corporate setting, passion is important. It is with passion that many people have made significant contributions to society, without which we would have all been poorer. The heart knows what the mind does not. Passion comes from the heart and can lead human beings to great heights.

However, sometimes emotions obscure the way and disconnect us from our goals. Passion without reason can lead to extremism, which can be harmful.

Reason is vital because it is logical and stable; it plays an important part in bringing balance.

Ibn Arabi says, "See with both eyes—reason and passion." This will bring out the best results, both in corporate endeavor and in private life.

Focusing on the Important Matters

Do not focus on insignificant things.

ᐶ **Sufi Saying**

In his book *When You Hear Hoofbeats, Think of a Zebra*, Shems Friedlander writes of a soldier who is wounded in battle. Instead of focusing on how he can save his own life, the soldier wants to find out the insignificant details of how he was wounded. He wants to know who the archer was, what he looked like, and where he was standing when he released the arrow. He wants to know the type of bow and the length of the arrow. As he searches for all these answers, the wounded man dies. Sufis recommend concentrating on the essence, not on the form.

In this fast-paced society, achieving balance requires that we organize our lives around key priorities and focus on what matters the most. Planning helps to identify what is really important; it helps distinguish the important things from the non-essentials. If we look after the important things with care, the less important things will fall into place. When the big stuff is looked after, the small stuff is a piece of cake.

Similarly, in the age of information overload it is important not to get caught up reading material that is insignificant. Having clarity of goals helps us to decide whether the information is going to help us to accomplish these goals. We are able to pull out the essence from the endless information and paper that come to us every day.

In the corporate world it is important to spend time in areas that can provide the greatest contributions, thereby increasing our value to others and to ourselves. We need the art of not only getting things done, but also of getting things undone—in other words, the art of eliminating the non-essentials. The key is to have a tight set of priorities and stick to them.

Action Items

❧ Focus on the most important things and eliminate the non-essentials. Do less, and focus on the really significant things that are consistent with your vision.

❧ Remember that real success is holistic and includes work, family, health, spirituality, and learning. Therefore, schedule time for these important aspects of your life.

❧ Maintain a balance between passion and reason. Use the right and left sides of your brain.

❧ Learn to say "no" to the unimportant things.

❧ Start your day sixty minutes earlier, devoting your newly gained hour to meditation, exercise, and reading inspirational material in equal measure. This will give you a headstart on the day. Go to sleep an hour earlier to make up for lost sleep.

10

Savoring the Path

❦

Every Breath Is Our Life

Being a Child of the Moment

Savoring the Path

❦

Ask the following questions:

❧ Do I savor every moment and enjoy the small successes of my life?

❧ Do I go with the flow and still stay on purpose?

❧ Do I avoid postponing my happiness?

❧ Do I worry about things that have not yet happened?

Every Breath Is Our Life

*Every breath taken in replenishes life,
and once let go of, it gives joy to the
soul. So each breath counts as two
blessings, and each blessing requires
thanksgiving.*

❧ **Sa'di, from his poem *Gulistan***

With every breath we take in, we are given new life. What is the new self that we experience at each breath? The new self of the moment is God's constant, never-ending renewal of the self's creation. At each moment of our existence, a new self arrives to us from God, just as, in this body, a new breath arrives. We can be happy—not tomorrow, not yesterday, but moment to moment, beginning now.

Yesterday and tomorrow are only relevant because we are alive today. Yesterday exists only in our memory. We cannot re-create yesterday. It is gone forever. The Sufis ask, "What is yesterday but today's memory? What is tomorrow but today's dream?"

Sufis believe in making the most of unfolding life and not worrying about the past or the future. Worry is a heavy cloud that covers the sunshine of today. Believe in the beauty and power of now!

The stars move, the tides ebb and flow in their own time, and the seasons pass one after the other. Why are we in such a rush? Go with the flow and treasure life moment by moment. Everything is perfect as it is.

In a corporate setting, goal setting is very important. It gives a sense of direction and also allows for the proper allocation of time. Goals are our drivers and energizers, and we need to treasure them as our success companions. However, we need to act now to make our goals a reality.

What is tomorrow, but today's dream? Who knows about it? Why worry about it? There are so many variables regarding tomorrow which may never be. So why spend energy living for tomorrow? The future is not something we travel, but rather something we build by living to our potential today.

All we have is today. It is a priceless day. Seize it! Live it fully! Today well-lived makes yesterday a good dream and tomorrow full of hope. Life is what happens day by day, moment by moment.

Direction is important, but flexibility allows us to live fully each day without straying from our vision.

Being a Child of the Moment

*The Sufi acts according to whatever is
most fitting to the moment.*

❧ **Amr Ibn Uthman al-Makki, Sufi writer**

The true Sufi lives in the constant awareness that the self is nothing but what he is at the present moment. Since each present moment is unique, each moment of the self is unique. Silent and persevering remembrance of God in gratitude for each breath takes us to our ultimate goal of union with God. Heedlessness is when we ignore the wealth and beauty of each breath.

All that ever happened or will ever happen to us is contained in this moment; this very moment is perfect and powerful—there is no need to wait for another. The past and future only exist in our mind. We really only have the moment and the rest is neither here nor there. The Sufi is the child of the moment.

We can all learn from a child who is fully present in everything he does. It is we who then try to change that state of being by reminding him of his past mistakes or tempting him with future rewards for "specific responsible behavior."

In a corporate setting we make each and every day at work a perfect day. It is what we make of the day that matters. The process is the most important thing in the journey. Most people postpone living, waiting for the perfect moment to live fully and be happy. The moment is now! It is about letting go, about yielding. We live our corporate life in this manner by putting our mind, body, and heart into the task at hand.

One way to live fully is to go with the flow. If we go with the current, life becomes effortless and the whole river is our helper. If we go against the current, we really have to toil. Going with the flow brings us harmony with the universe. There are things that the universe knows that we don't. The Universal Knowledge knows the end of all ends. The key is to utilize the flow of life and circumstances to assist us in reaching our goals and purpose in life.

Flowing water is soft yet powerful. It surrenders to gravity without resistance by adapting to its environment. Water reveals an effective way of going with the flow and letting go. As Bruce Lee once said, "The less effort, the faster and more powerful you will be."

Savoring the Path

*The path has no value when you have
arrived.*

❧ Sufi Saying

We are always becoming. The beauty, however, is in the being, not in the becoming. When we savor the challenges and struggles of life, they become wonderful experiences. So often we are waiting to overcome our challenges and forget to enjoy the process. We are always trying to get to some place else, not realizing that the beauty is in the journey.

The challenges are always going to be there. If we admire someone and try to put ourselves in his shoes, we will find that even this person has his challenges. It is a never-ending process, and we need to thank God for it. For without these challenges and struggles, the valuable lessons of life could not be learned.

In our corporate lives the path is the destiny. Once we arrive, the path has no value. So let us not cease to savor the journey. It is exciting, challenging, and invigorating. It is a place for continuing growth, experience, and wisdom. Value the path, learn from it, and apply the learning to future endeavors. Each time we stumble or struggle, we need to ask ourselves: What have I learned from this and how can it help me in the future? There are no failures, only lessons.

Action Items

❧ Savor every moment and enjoy the small successes of life.

❧ Focus on what is right in front of you to the exclusion of everything else. Do not let your thoughts dwell in the past or the future. Be fully present in whatever you do.

❧ Live today as if you were to die tomorrow. Live in the moment—it may be your last. Do not postpone things that you want to do.

❧ Go with the flow without losing sight of your purpose. Say to yourself that the circumstances in your life are the universe's way of helping you reach your destiny.

❧ Schedule time to do the things you love to do.

11

Taming Our Ego

❦

Giving up Self to Taste Greatness

❦

Ask the following questions:

❧ Do I possess positive pride or am I egotistical?

❧ How do I react to negative comments directed towards me? Do I take things personally and become defensive?

❧ Do I realize my mistakes and admit them?

❧ How do I treat my colleagues, customers, and suppliers?

❧ Do I share the limelight with my team?

Giving up Self to Taste Greatness

When did I become less by dying.

❦ **Rumi**

Rumi uses the word "dying" to imply the killing of the ego. Each time we kill the ego, we rise spiritually.

We are all gifted in some way, so there is no point in putting others down. Nasruddin the Sufi tells a story of a proud grammarian on a boat ride who was ridiculing a boat driver who did not know grammar. He insulted the driver by saying half his life had been wasted. Then the tide rose and the boat was sinking. At that point it became apparent that the grammarian did not know how to swim and *his* whole life was wasted.

Rabi'a the Sufi saint, used to promote love as the basis of all spiritual progress. For her where there was love, there would be respect and an absence of negative pride.

In a corporate setting positive pride is a great quality to have. It enables people to excel and to do great things for the betterment of society. It is the zest and gumption to go out and give your best.

Egotism, or negative pride, on the other hand makes us narrow and unable to see life beyond self. We achieve "success" at the expense of others and belittle and exploit them in the process. We rely on our wealth and power as opposed to our authentic self. Such an attitude injures us as well as our work.

If we want to accomplish great things, we can never do so if we are egotistical. It can only happen through positive pride and by taming the ego. Many great works done by entrepreneurs, scientists, and artists happened because these people were driven by positive pride and forgot themselves in the bigger purpose of their work. The subject disappeared in the object.

If we find ourselves becoming defensive or taking things personally, these are signs of our ego creeping in. When we share the limelight with people who help us achieve the success and admit our mistakes when we make them, these are signs of positive pride. Bayazid Al-Bistami, a Sufi saint, says, "When does a man become a man? When he knows his own mistakes and hurries to correct them."

The Sufi Inayat Khan says, "All great musicians, Beethoven, Wagner, and many others, who have left the world a work that will always be treasured, would not have been able to do so if they had not forgotten themselves (ego) in their work." These people were able to transform themselves just like the metamorphosis of a caterpillar into a butterfly. This self-transformation happens through the annihilation of the ego from which the magnificent new form emerges.

136

Action Items

❧ Catch yourself when you become egotistical and immediately correct yourself.

❧ Always be thankful for gifts that you have been blessed with by which you achieve your success. Remind yourself that you have been created and are not the creator. Whatever success you have is by the grace of the Divine.

❧ Stay away from the limelight and focus on your goals.

❧ Share your success with the people who help you attain it.

❧ Remember that your treatment of others is a reflection of you.

12

Igniting Our Spirituality

⁂

Taking the Pearl

Playing to One Tune

Meditating Regularly

Removing the Dust

Opening the Inner Eye

⁂

Ask the following questions:

- What is spirituality? How is it connected to corporate life?

- Is every employee in tune with the corporate music?

- What is the "spirit" of the corporation?

- Am I seeing things as they are or as I am?

- Do I have too much clutter blocking my inspiration, intuition, enthusiasm, and creativity?

Taking the Pearl

*Having seen the form, you are unaware
of the meaning. If you are wise, pick out
the pearl from the shell.*

❧ **Rumi**

Spirituality is esoteric, not exoteric. It is not what is apparent but what is hidden. The walnut has a shell, a seed, and the oil. The shell symbolizes the exoteric; the seed, the esoteric; and the oil, the essence that permeates the whole walnut. The Sufis focus on the esoteric, on the essence that is inside and hidden. They integrate the exoteric, that which is evident and outside, with the esoteric, that which is subtle and inside.

Examine the corporate soul—why it exists, what its real purpose is. We must ask ourselves what the real reason is for doing the work we are doing. Understanding this important fact brings clarity. Many difficult corporate issues arise from a lack of clarity.

As business people, when we have absolute clarity, we can transcend petty issues that consume much of our energy. As J.C. Penny says, "The letter killeth, the spirit giveth life." The spirit is the essence, the rest is details. Do not settle for the shell, but pick out the pearl.

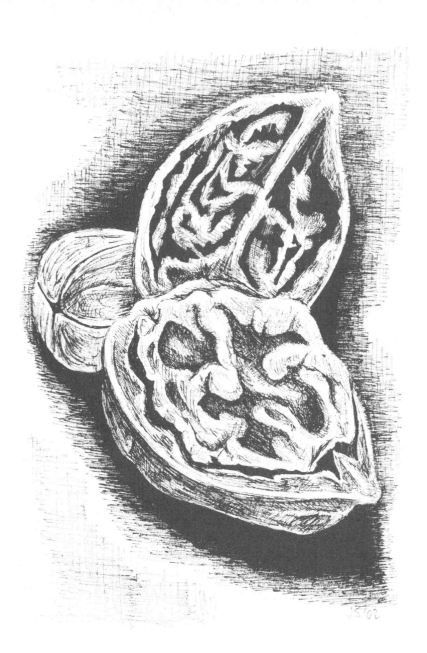

The walnut's shell symbolizes the exoteric; the seed, the esoteric; and the oil, the essence that permeates the whole walnut.

Playing to One Tune

Life as a whole in all its aspects is one single music, and spiritual attainment is to tune oneself to the harmony of this perfect music.

❧ **Sufi Inayat Khan**

Sufis look at life, people, and the environment as parts of the Oneness of God. When we truly understand this, we are in harmony. We are playing the same music as the rest of creation.

Similarly, we have to ensure that everyone in our organization is playing the same music. In other words, we must pursue harmony and a shared vision. This propels the company forward, as all the energies are directed to one end, resulting in a synergy of effort.

Like an orchestra we can have diverse players with different instruments, but they all need to synchronize to the same tune. This tune would be impossible to hear were it not for the contribution of all the players.

Identify the single music in your corporation. Ask yourself if there is a commitment from everyone to play this music. If not, it is essential to invest time to get this in order; otherwise, there will be disjointed efforts limiting the corporation's progress.

The corporate leader, like a conductor of an orchestra ensures the team is playing to one tune.

Meditating Regularly

Meditation opens the door to spiritual enlightenment.

❧ **Sufi Saying**

Meditation means sitting quietly, doing nothing, and being empty of all thoughts. It is a vehicle that allows us to connect with our spiritual core.

Some psychologists say that we have as many as 60,000 thoughts a day and that these can have a very stressful impact on the physical body. Meditation relaxes and stills the mind of its endless chatter and clutter. It can be practiced in many different ways, but the ultimate purpose is attaining spiritual enlightenment.

To meditate, we must be comfortable with silence. For many of us, though, silence can be an uncomfortable experience. Why is silence important? If we want to connect with the Divine Light that permeates the universe, then we need to tune into it. This can only happen through silence. Being in close touch with nature relaxes us and puts us in the mood for silence and meditation.

145

In the corporate world it is work, work, work. Why are we working so hard? Sufis say stop working and do nothing, even doodle for a while. When we spend time in silence we get a better perspective of life. We are better able to focus and direct our energies to achieving corporate success. A quiet mind is powerful. The practice of meditation will help us relax and become intuitive, thereby increasing our productivity and corporate performance.

We need to prepare both our body and mind for meditation. We prepare our body by not abusing it through harmful habits such as taking drugs, smoking and drinking alcohol. We exercise regularly and have healthy eating habits to get the body ready for meditation We get the mind ready for meditation by being in the present moment and excluding the past and future from our minds. The more relaxed we are the better our chances of accomplishing this.

Concentration and focus are invaluable in corporate life. They allow us to be more accurate and to accomplish ever more important tasks. The practice of regular meditation increases our capacity to concentrate.

If we observe a spider spin its web, we can appreciate the concentration required to perform this intricate task.

The great Shibli went to visit the illustrious master, Thauri. The master was sitting so still that not a hair moved. Shibli asked, "Where did you learn such still-ness?" Thauri replied, "From a cat. He was watching a mouse hole with even greater concentration than you have seen in me!"

Removing the Dust

*Soul is like a clear mirror; the body is
dust on it. Beauty in us is not perceived;
for we are under the dust.*

☙ Rumi

The truth is obscured when we have 'dust' in us, just as, when we look at a mirror that has dust, we cannot see clearly the full picture.

The Sufis believe that removing the dust is a cleansing process which should be undertaken if we wish to attain spiritual success. We need to seek forgiveness and repentance. Once our soul is cleansed, we will be very cautious not to err again, just as we would be very careful not to stain a clean shirt but would not worry about staining our dirty overalls. We must aim to clean the soul and avoid staining it.

In corporate life we may not be seeing the full picture because we are dealing with unresolved issues from the past or have preconceived notions that may cloud reality. This inhibits intuition and limits our potential.

One way to prevent impurities from obscuring our "mirror" is to be aware of our actions and thoughts. The more self-aware we are, the more vigilant we become and the less "dust" we gather.

The other way to prevent impurities creeping in is through taming our ego. Rumi gives the analogy of the iron ore that is full of impurities when it is dug out of the ground. After it is put through the furnace it burns the impurities and comes out as iron. Similarly in a human the death of the ego is the birth of a pure soul which keeps the dust away.

Leaders play an important part in creating an enabling environment that encourages a positive feedback system to help the team remove the dust.

Opening the Inner Eye

You need the inner eye to see and experience spirituality.

ॐ Sufi Saying

The word "spirituality" comes from the word "spirit," which is synonymous with the word "soul." The purpose of a Sufi is to be in tune with that spirit. He believes that everything we do should emanate from spirituality. We should have singularity of purpose and act in accordance with it. Clarity and consistency prevent stress and frustration.

See what appears to be non-existent—the soul. Open your inner eye and the mystery of life will unfold. Just as the owl is blind to daylight, we are blind to the spiritual world, unable to see phenomena that really do exist.

Rumi explains that the season of spring comes to our fragrant trees with an offering. He says that although the spring is hidden you can look at the effect it has on the gardens that are dead. It resurrects them back to life. He invites the spring of love to come into the garden of the soul and awaken the spirit. When our spirit is awakened, we open our inner eyes.

Remember that everything cannot be seen through the eyes, smelled with the nose, heard with the ears, or felt with the skin. Can we see the air that we breathe? Can we see the fragrance of a flower? Say to the embryo in the womb that there is a beautiful world outside; it will not believe you.

Being open and vigilant to what is around us enables us to see things below the surface. If we are among those corporate people who do things automatically and mechanically, we are probably missing not just the intangibles, but quite possibly even the tangible things; we are oblivious to the meaning behind each activity we are performing. It is like the fish that has lived its entire life in water and, one day, wants to know where the water is.

Take some time off from rituals and spend time in reflection, developing the "inner eye." The inner eye sees people in their essence and spirit. Deep down we all have a soul that is pure.

If we, as corporate people, looked at all our colleagues, suppliers, and customers with the inner eye, we could have excellent relationships, making our work environment more pleasant and productive. Corporations would benefit because teamwork would be enhanced through this compassionate approach.

The fish has lived in the ocean all its life and is asking
"Where is the water?"

Action Items

❧ Know your corporate soul—the real reason for the corporation's existence.

❧ Practice noticing things most people fail to notice. You do this by being alert and by concentrating.

❧ Meditate for 20 minutes regularly, and see how it can increase your energy and tranquility.

❧ Look for the underlying meaning in events that happen at work today. Try to focus on the essence of a particular issue, and don't become caught up in the details.

❧ Eliminate self-limiting concepts that block spirituality by focusing on your ultimate vision and goals.

13

Understanding Life and Death

❧

Our Boat of Life Is Rushing By

Timelessness Is in All of Us

We Cannot Extend Our Journey of Life

Our Life Is Short

❧

Ask the following questions:

- Am I prepared for death?

- Do I realize that wealth is important but cannot extend my life?

- Am I losing sight of the bigger purpose in life?

- How long is my corporate life? How can I make my contributions in the corporate world permanent?

Our Boat of Life
Is Rushing By

*In a boat rushing on a fast-running
creek, it seems as if the trees on the
bank are rushing by. What seems to be
changing around us is rather the speed
of our craft leaving this world.*

❧ Rumi

The Sufis believe that everything in creation is a process. You cannot rush a flower to bloom, nor can you rush a seed to come to fruition. The natural processes are pre-determined and cannot be altered. Similarly, we need to slow down and not force things to happen. We need to accustom ourselves to the natural order of things.

In our corporate life, going fast and being busy are not necessarily recipes for effectiveness and success. Success requires knowing the reality, having a direction, and heading there. If we feel "the trees on the bank" are rushing by, what is changing is rather the time we have left in this world.

When we are living in a fast-paced world, everything seems rushed, and it is easy to blame the environment

What is changing is the speed of our craft leaving this
world and not the trees on the bank

and circumstances for our rushed lives. However, the reality is that it is up to us as to how fast we want to go. We have the choice to stop to spend time in reflection and contemplation.

By slowing down, we are able to differentiate between reality and illusion, and we have a better chance of gaining that indispensable sense of perspective and direction in life. What good is it to go fast if we are traveling in the wrong direction? We only get to the wrong place faster. It is better to go slowly, but to head in the right direction; we get there slowly but surely.

When we slow down and remain centered, there seems to be more time. In reality, time cannot increase, but our sense of anticipation is heightened and our total devotion to the tasks we set for ourselves is achieved to the point that we feel we have more time.

Timelessness Is in All of Us

We are timeless and placeless.

❧ Sufi Saying

The earth drinks water from the sky, receives sunlight, and gives life to plants and herbs. Animals eat plants, humans eat animals. Eventually, humans are absorbed into the earth. And so, the circle of life continues.

The ocean waves rise and fall and rise again. The seasons come and go and come again. All things happen in their own good time. Our soul too is timeless, as it is not restricted to our physical life on earth.

Corporations can be timeless in the contributions they make to the world. These contributions can last far beyond the corporate life span. Scientists who find cures for deadly diseases, those who contribute time and money for the less fortunate in the world, and those who work hard to bring about world peace are examples of services beyond a single corporate life span.

In the corporate setting, this message is appropriate in that it reminds us of our dependence on others who have left this world but created things that we enjoy. As Rumi says, "Your lamp was lit from another lamp." Everything we do rests on the efforts of others. We have risen to succeed on the shoulders of those who have contributed before us. We realize that their contributions to our success, although unseen, made it easier for us to succeed.

We have a responsibility to care for the environment and leave something behind for future generations before we depart. A day will come when we will be given an escape to the new world. As Rumi says, "The day you were born, a ladder was set up to help you escape from this world."

We Cannot Extend Our Journey of Life

The world is like a caravanserai with two doors: entering by one door, I pass out through the other. I am sunk in heedless sleep and know of nothing; I shall die whether I will it or not. Be I beggar or king...willy-nilly I must in the end be parted from all that I have. Though I be Alexander, this transitory world will one day provide a shroud for all my Alexander-like glory.

✧ Fariduddin Attar, great Sufi Persian poet

The Sufis understand that death will greet us one day and that we do not have control over the timing of our death. What we do have control over is the time we have while we are alive. Just as the flower realizes that it has no control over when it blooms and fades, it gives of its beauty and fragrance while it is blooming and without hesitation.

Our life on this planet is much like a long dream. When we are dreaming, we are fully involved with the drama. But when we wake up and realize that it was a dream, we

162

forget about it within a very short time. Similarly, our lives with all the melodrama will one day end, and the physical life will become like a dream.

Corporations too have a limited life span. Times change, economies evolve, and corporations fade away, but the contributions they make can last forever. Khalil Gibran aptly says, "Give while the season of giving is here, so that your coffer is not empty when you die."

Our Life Is Short

We have four seasons to live,
three may be gone.

❦ **Sufi Saying**

It is said we have four seasons to live—spring, summer, fall, and winter. But three seasons may already be over. Time, as we know it in this world, is very short, like the blinking of the eye.

We postpone living, as if life goes on forever. We postpone spirituality, thinking we can handle it in our old age where we think we will have more time. But what is old age? Who can assure us of this old age? We can plan for 50 years, but we do not know what will happen in the next second.

We need to integrate our spiritual identity with everything we do in the physical world. The way we walk, talk, eat, sleep, conduct our business, and interact with our family and friends can all be integrated and reflect our spirituality.

Life is a precious gift—a gift that comes with responsibility. With this blessing we are expected to use our talents to make our world, including our corporate environment, a better place and to live an ethical, well-balanced life.

This gives us a sense of urgency in our corporate lives and the desire to address the really important issues in our lives without procrastinating.

Action Items

❦ Live every day as if it were your last. Make a contribution that lasts beyond your lifetime.

❦ Make time for the most important things in your life— family, spirituality, and health.

❦ Taking a long-term perspective helps to differentiate between reality and illusion. Ask yourself: How important will this issue or decision be 50 years from now?

14

Experiencing God in Corporate Life

❧

Viewing God With Our Limited Vision

God Has an Open-Door Policy

Discovering God's Immanence in Our Corporate Life

❧

Ask the following questions:

❧ What has God got to do with my corporate life?

❧ Do I take notice of God on my team?

❧ How does God make my corporate life more meaningful and successful?

❧ What are the signposts of God, and why are they important in my corporate life?

Viewing God With Our Limited Vision

Trying to understand God is to fathom the sun with the understanding of the lamp.

✤ Sufi Saying

The Sufis believe it is impossible to view God with our limited vision, but we can experience Him through the spirit. A Sufi devotes his life to the preparation for this spiritual experience.

Taj Kavi, a contemporary Sufi, explains, "God, before birth I was in You. After birth, You resided in me. So what is the difference between You and me? When You puffed, I was born. When I puffed, nothing happened!"

Most people claim to know God by their own limited vision. Similarly, the worldview of corporate people is limited to one's experiences and knowledge, which may not be totally accurate or exhaustive.

We see the corporate world based on our understanding. We see the issues and complexities based on our past experiences and outlook.

We begin the process of expanding our horizons by accepting and realizing that there is more than that which meets the eye.

We have to remind ourselves that all limits are set in our minds. If we break through these imaginary ceilings, we are free to fly higher and experience things far beyond our imagination.

Ibn Arabi says, "God is your mirror in which you contemplate yourself, and you are His mirror in which He contemplates His divine attributes."

God Has an Open-Door Policy

"Come, Come, Come, Come
Whoever you are! Wanderer,
Worshipper, lover of leaving,
This is not a caravan of despair,
It doesn't matter if you've broken
Your vows a thousand times, still
And yet again come!"

❧ Rumi

Rumi describes God's unlimited mercy and open-door policy. God never closes His door. Whenever we decide to turn towards Him, He will receive us—even if we have broken our vows a thousand times.

Sufis believe that holding grudges against others is harmful to spiritual progress. Forgiveness is an act that releases energy and benefits the forgiver as well as the forgiven. Any anger or hurt that we let fester in our hearts impedes our spiritual growth.

From a corporate point of view this Sufi message helps us to understand that we need to forgive others, as well as ourselves. We may decide not to work with someone who is incompetent, but we can still forgive him. This eliminates negative energy from our personal and corporate midst.

As leaders, we sometimes have to turn a blind eye to minor shortcomings of our team. If we do not do so, we may discourage them from trying again. We will breed compliance instead of creativity and risk taking. As a result, our corporation may stagnate instead of growing.

When we do not forgive, we lose our centeredness, and this affects our corporate performance. We do not waste our energy on ill will. Rather, we use this energy for fulfilling our real corporate purpose.

Hostile competition in the corporate world can lead to festering grudges which can be destructive, as they are never-ending and eventually lead to our own downfall. We seek collaboration wherever possible and strive to conduct our business in an ethical and dignified manner. In the long run, this brings the best results.

Discovering God's Immanence in Our Corporate Life

*God is greater than the universe, yet He
is found in the heart of a believer.*

❧ **Sufi Saying**

Our hearts are temples that house God. God is both transcendent and immanent.

A Sufi aims to prepare his soul to house God and to be in touch with Him at all times. He works at being worthy of this privilege. Divine grace will come to a pure soul. Just as a farmer prepares the soil for planting, so too we prepare our soul for God's mercy.

In our corporation, God becomes present through our ethics and principles. When we understand our motives and establish strong ethical principles on which we operate, we connect to this source. These principles are the hub from which our corporation operates. The immanence of God's presence lies in His creation—our team. God is one, and we are all part of that one. When we work as a team in a unified way towards noble goals, we invite God into our lives.

The Sufis say that everything in creation is a signpost to the Oneness of God. When we see a beautiful swan, or a bird flying, or the moonlight, we are looking at signs of God. When we respect God's creatures, be it human, plant, or animal, we are respecting God.

Muhamed Ibn Wasi says, "I've never seen a single thing without seeing God in it."

Sufis rely on God just like a newborn baby relies on his mother to fulfill all his needs. The bond between a mother and child is one of love and faith, and so also is ours with God.

If we have invited God into our corporation, then respect and love will permeate throughout, bringing teamwork, harmony, and higher productivity. The industrialist Henry J. Kaiser said, "Use the great powers that you can tap through faith in God and the hidden energies of your soul and sub-conscious mind." If we have the faith, God's power comes to our aid in mysterious ways.

A friend of mine who is president of a large North American hotel chain starts his day with the following prayer: "God make my day such that I make a significant contribution to the lives of all the people I lead." This is an example of inviting God to be by our side in accomplishing worthwhile corporate goals.

Look at the beauty around you. Everything in creation
is a signpost to the Oneness of God.

Action Items

❧ Be God-conscious at all times. Imagine that He is present in all your corporate activities.

❧ Acknowledge that everyone is a signpost of God. Respect for others is respect for God.

❧ Keep a big heart and overlook minor shortcomings. See the good in others.

❧ Expand your horizon. Be alert and aware that there is more than what is apparent.

Revisiting the Corporate Sufi Principles

Throughout this book we have been encouraged to apply the corporate Sufi principles in our daily lives. Some of the important practical messages that we have covered are:

Finding Our Purpose

- ❧ Once we find our life mission, the one thing we need to do is to fuse it with all of our activities—personal and corporate. By so doing, we unleash our potential and find fulfillment on our journey.

- ❧ We have clarity with respect to the big picture which keeps us focused and enthusiastic. We never lose sight of our vision which is our driving force.

Embracing a Principle-Centered Approach

❧ We apply the Sufi principles to corporate life, thereby creating meaning and fulfillment in our work lives. The Sufi principles include listening to and trusting the voice of our conscience and working with integrity, principles, and respect.

❧ We have a social conscience, and we ensure that our corporate work creates a better society all round. We do not engage in any activity that is detrimental to the overall well-being of society or the environment.

Making a Difference

❧ We are non-judgmental and believe in the inherent talents of all people, including ourselves, and are able to tap into the best of everyone. We do this by eliminating fear and creating an enabling environment where our team's skills are given the best chance to flourish.

❧ We strive for collaboration and synergy in our corporate lives, as opposed to competition. Through this approach we create positive energy that is a source of power and strength. We are true leaders, having a knack for finding the right people for our team, and are able to motivate and inspire the team around a shared vision.

❧ It is not just what we have that matters; rather, the value of our lives is determined by who we are and what we give. We treat life as a precious gift and use this gift to give and to make a difference.

Embracing Life-Long Learning

❧ We learn from cradle to grave. We learn from all, including nature which offers immense wisdom. We know that, in order to succeed in life, competence is the key which comes from life-long learning.

❧ We reward team players who engage in life-long learning.

Having Faith in the Unknown

❧ Just like the Sufi who does not fear anything in his pursuit of finding the truth, we do not fear the unknown. We are willing to take risks and to persevere in realizing our dreams.

❧ We do not worry about conventional wisdom but are constantly finding innovative and creative ways of doing things.

Persevering

❧ We never, never give up! We persist until we succeed in achieving what we believe in.

❧ Perseverance and patience go hand in hand.

Being Effective Leaders

- We are role models inspiring our team through our examples.
- We eliminate insecurities by trusting and believing in the inherent abilities and gifts of team members.
- We are result-driven, not task-based.
- We empower our team—we do not overpower them.

Keeping a Positive Attitude

- We keep confident expectations. What we expect is what we invite into our lives.
- We are solution-oriented, not problem-focused.
- We give people the benefit of the doubt.
- We do not worry about criticism. We believe in doing our best and leaving the rest.

Balancing Our Lives

- Real success is holistic and caters to our body, mind, and soul. We allocate our time wisely and do not compromise a tight set of priorities, which brings us balance and synergy.
- We try to start the day early with a dose of twenty minutes each of meditation, exercise, and reading inspirational material.

Savoring The Path

❧ We know that our destiny lies in the path we walk. We love the challenges and hurdles along the way because they enhance our strength and tenacity.

❧ We regard each day as the most important day of our lives. Thus, every day—every moment—is a gift that we cherish and savor. We go with the flow without taking our eyes off our goals.

Taming Our Ego

❧ We strive for positive pride and shun egotism.

❧ We let the subject disappear in the object by letting the self disappear in the higher purpose of our work.

❧ We accept our shortcomings. We do not have a need to become defensive or take things personally.

Igniting Our Spirituality

❧ We meditate regularly to connect to our spirituality, inviting intuition, creativity, enthusiasm, and passion into our lives.

❧ We practice creating "one music" with everyone in our corporation to that each person contributes to it like a symphony.

❧ We make spirituality the centerpiece of our lives, including our corporate lives, so that 24 hours of our day are grounded in spirituality.

❧ We know the corporate soul—the real reason for the corporation's existence.

Understanding Life and Death

❧ We realize that there is a beginning and an end to everything in life. Every beginning is an end of the old; and every end a beginning of the new.

❧ When we die, we do not take what we have, but rather, what we gave.

Experiencing God in Corporate Life

❧ We know that all success ultimately is by the grace of God. Hard work and struggle pay dividends, but without grace we cannot go too far. We invite God into our corporate lives and make Him our partner in everything we do.

❧ We become co-creators with God by creating something beautiful in this world through our work.

❧ We see God in all. We understand that everything and everybody is a signpost to the Oneness of God.

By applying the principles of teamwork, lifelong learning, purposeful work, effective leadership, focus, perseverance, and tapping into intuition and spirituality, the corporation is bound to produce better results and increase its profitability.

The Sufi principles are universal and practical. They are founded on love and act as a bridge between our personal and corporate lives. If these principles are implemented by one and all, the corporate world could be a more happy, peaceful, and loving place where each person is given the space and the opportunity to flower to his or her potential and to contribute to society and to the world. Our corporate lives will then be materially rewarding, as well as spiritually enriching.

Good luck on your journey. May you be guided by the Divine Light every step of the way.

God bless you.

Azim

Bibliography

The Sufi quotes in this book are mostly translated works from different languages. These quotes have been taken from some of the following books.

Ad-Darqawi, Shaikh Al-'Arabi. *Letters of a Sufi Master*. London: Perennial Books, 1973.

Angha, Ali Nader Shah. *Of Religion*. California: Riverside, 2000.

Angha, Ali Nader Shah. *Sufism, the Reality of Religion*. Washington, DC, M.T.O. Shahmaghsoudi Publications, 1998.

Arberry, Arthur John. *The Doctrine of the Sufis*. Great Britain: Cambridge University Press, 1966.

Attar, Farid al-Din (Translated by A.J. Arberry). *Muslim Saints and Mystics*. Great Britain: Penguin Books Ltd., 1966.

Bach, Richard. *Illusions*. Great Britain: William Heinemann, 1977.

Bach, Richard. *Jonathan Livingston Seagull.* Great Britain: Turnstone Press, 1972.

Bakhtiar, Laleh. *Sufi.* Canada: Thames and Hudson, 1987.

Bayat, Mojdeh and Mohammad Ali Jamnia. *Tales from the Land of the Sufis.* Boston: Shambhala, 1994.

Bilgrami, H. H. *Glimpses of Iqbal's Mind and Thought.* Lahore: Sh. Muhammad Ashraf, 1966.

Burckhardt, Titus (Translated by D.M.Matheson). *Introduction to Sufism.* San Francisco: HarperCollins, 1993.

Burckhardt, Titus. *Letters of a Sufi Master: The Shaykh ad-Darqawi.* Louisville, KY: Fons Vitae, 1998.

Carlson, Richard. *Don't Sweat the Small Stuff...at Work.* New York: Hyperion, 1998.

Champy, James. *Reengineering Management.* New York: Harper Business, 1995.

Chittick, William. *The Sufi Path of Knowledge* Ibn al-Arabi. State of NY Press Albany, 1989.

Chittick, William C. *Sufism: A Short Introduction.* Oxford: Oneworld Publications, 2000.

Corbin, Henry (Translated by Nancy Pearson). *The Man of Light in Iranian Sufism.* Lebanon, NY: Omega Publications, 1994.

Covey, Stephen R. *The 7 Habits of Highly Effective People*. New York: Simon & Schuster, 1989.

Covey, Stephen R. *First Things First*. New York: Simon and Schuster, 1994.

Dauphinais, G. William, Grady Means and Colin Price. *Wisdom of the CEO*. New York: John Wiley & Sons, Inc., 2000.

Davis, F. Hadland. *The Persian Mystics, Rumi, Jalalu'din*. Lahore: Ashraf Press, 1973.

Dayao, Dinna Louise C. *Asian Business Wisdom*. Singapore: John Wiley & Sons, Inc. (Asia), 2000.

De Mello, Anthony. *One Minute Wisdom*. New York: Doubleday & Company, Inc., 1968.

Dolnick, Barrie. *Executive Mystic*. New York: Harper Business, 1998.

Ed-Din, Abu Barkr Siraj. *The Book of Certainty*. New York: Samuel Weiser, 1974.

Ernst, Carl W. *Teachings of Sufism*. Boston: Shambhala Publications Inc., 1999.

Ernst, Carl W. *The Shambhala Guide to Sufism*. Boston: Shambhala Publications Inc., 1997.

Freke, Timothy. *The Wisdom of the Sufi Sages.* Great Britain: Journey Editions, an imprint of Periphus Editions (UK) Ltd., 1998.

Friedlander, Shems. *When You Hear Hoofbeats, Think of a Zebra.* California: Mazda, 1987.

Gibran, Kahlil. *The Prophet.* New York: Alfred A. Knopf, 1923

Harvey, Andrew and Eryk Hanut. *Perfume of the Desert (Inspirations from Sufi Wisdom).* Quest Books, Wheaton, Il 1999.

Harvey, Andrew. *Teachings of Rumi.* Boston: Shambhala Publications, Inc., 1999.

Heider, John. *The Tao of Leadership.* Atlanta: Humanics New Age, 1985.

Hendricks, Gay and Kate Ludeman. *The Corporate Mystic.* New York; Bantam Books, 1996.

Hill, Napoleon. *Think and Grow Rich.* New York: Fawcett Crest, 1983.

Imam Ali ibn Abu Talib. *Nahjul Balagha Peak of Eloquence.* New York: Tahrike Tarsile Qur'an Inc. Fifth US Edition, 1986.

Jalal al-Din Rumi, Maulana (Translated by Coleman Barks with John Moyne). *The Essential Rumi*. New York: HarperCollins, 1995.

Jalal al-Din Rumi, Maulana (Translated by William Chittick). *The Sufi Path of Love: The Spiritual Teachings of Rumi*. Albany: State of New York Press, 1983.

Khan, Inayat. *Music*. New Delhi: Sufi Publishing Company Ltd, 1973.

Khan, Inayat. *The Wisdom of Sufism*. Great Britain: Element Books Limited, 2000.

Khan, Khan Sahib Khaja. *The Secret of Ana'l-Haqq*. Pakistan, 1976.

Klein, Eric and John B. Izzo. *Awakening Corporate Soul*. Canada: Fairwinds Press, 1998.

Kolin, Azima Malita and Mafi, Maryam. *Rumi, Whispers of the Beloved*. London: HarperCollins, 1999.

Krass, Peter. *The Book of Leadership Wisdom*. New York: John Wiley & Sons, Inc., 1988.

Krass, Peter. *The Little Book of Business Wisdom*. New York: John Wiley & Sons, Inc., 2001.

Lakhani, Ali. *Sacred Web Series*. Vancouver, Self-Published, 1998-2002.

Lewin, Leonard (editor). *The Elephant in the Dark, and Other Writings on the Diffusion of Sufi Ideas in the West.* New York: E.P. Dutton & Co., Inc., 1976.

Lings, Martin. *A Sufi Saint of the Twentieth Century.* Berkeley and Los Angeles: University of California Press, 1973.

Lings, Martin. *What is Sufism?* Berkeley and Los Angeles: University of California Press, 1977.

McCarthy, R.J. *Al-Ghazali's Path to Sufism.* Louisville, KY: Fons Vitae, 2000.

Nasr, S.H. *Sufi Essays.* London: George Allen & Unwin, 1972.

Nicholson, Reynold. *Tabriz, Divani Shamsi on Rumi.* San Francisco: The Rainbow Bridge, 1973.

Nicholson, Reynold. *Rumi, Poet and Mystic.* Great Britain: Oneworld Publications, 1995.

Nicholson, Reynold. *Tales of Mystic Meaning.* Pakistan: Carvan Press, 2000.

Rumi, Jalaluddin. *Mystical Poems of Rumi.* Chicago and London: University of Chicago Press, 1968.

Rumi, Jalaluddin. *The Persian Mystics.* Lahore: Sh. Muhammad Ashraf, 1973.

Schimmel, Annemarie. *Deciphering the Signs of God.* Albany: State University of New York Press, 1994.

Schimmel, Annemarie. *Islam, An Introduction.* University of New York Press, 1992.

Schimmel, Annemarie. *My Soul is a Woman: The Feminine in Islam.* Continuum Publishing Co., 1999.

Schimmel, Annemarie. *Mystical Dimensions of Islam.* Chapel Hill: University of North Carolina Press, 1975.

Schimmel, Annemarie. *Mysticism in Islam.* California: University of Caroline Press, 1975.

Schimmel, Annemarie. *The Triumphant Sun: A Study of the Works of Jaluddin Rumi.* London: East-West, 1978.

Schwartz, David J. *The Magic of Thinking Big.* New York: Simon & Schuster, 1987.

Secretan, Lance H.K. *Reclaiming Higher Ground.* Toronto: Macmillan Canada, 1997.

Shah, Idries. *The Exploits of the Incomparable Mulla Nasrudin.* USA: E.P. Dutton & Co., Inc., 1972.

Shah, Idries. *The Magic Monastery.* New York: E.P. Dutton & Co. Inc., 1972.

Shah, Idries. *The Sufis.* New York: Doubleday & Company, 1964.

Shah, Idries. *The Way of the Sufi.* Great Britain: Penguin Books, 1974.

Shah, Idries. *Thinkers of the East.* Great Britain: Penguin Books, 1977.

Sharma, Robin S. *Leadership Wisdom from the Monk Who Sold His Ferrari.*

Smith, Margaret. *The Way of the Mystics: the early Christian mystics and the rise of the Sufis.* New York: Oxford University Press, 1978.

Stepaniants, Marietta T. *Sufi Wisdom.* State University of NY Press Albany, 1994.

Stoddart, William. *Sufism: The Mystical Doctrines and Methods of Islam.* Minnesota: Paragon Howard, 1985.

Tracy, Brain. *The 100 Absolutely Unbreakable Laws of Business Success.* San Francisco: Berrett-Koehler Publishers, Inc., 2000.

Waterhouse, Price. *Straight from the CEO.* New York: Simon & Schuster, 1998.

Whinfield, E. H., Masnavi i Ma'navi. *The Spiritual Couplets of Rumi.* London: Octagon Press, 1979.

Whinfield, E.H. *Teachings of Rumi.* Great Britain: The Octagon Press Ltd., 1979.

Winston, Stephanie. *The Organized Executive.* New York: Warner Books, 1994.

Keynote and Interactive Sessions with the Author

AZIM JAMAL
**Best-selling author and
professional inspirational speaker**

**He'll make you think. He'll make you laugh.
He'll make you cry.**

Drawing on his knowledge of business and spirituality, and his personal experiences, Azim energizes audiences with his thought-provoking and engaging style.

Azim Jamal's keynote addresses and interactive seminars have inspired audiences across the globe for nearly two decades. With an emphasis on balanced living, leadership, spirituality, living life fully, and happiness, his lively and electrifying addresses are customized to meet client objectives.

His themes include:

- ❧ Making a Difference
- ❧ Living to Your Potential
- ❧ Effective Leadership
- ❧ The Power of Balanced Living
- ❧ The Joy and Beauty of Giving
- ❧ How to Be Happy and Upbeat, No Matter What
- ❧ Spirituality

Azim's charismatic speaking style has motivated senior corporate executives, managers, entrepreneurs, professionals, community leaders, teachers, and students.

"Your seminar on The Leader in You at the Women and Wellness Conference organized by Safeway, United Way, Lindsay Park, Calgary Regional Health Authority and Agakhan Health Board was very well received and comments from participants included 'inspiring, dynamic speaking style, motivating, awesome, knowledgeable.' Thank you for your powerful presentation."

Rishma Manji, Chair, Aga Khan Health Board for the Prairies

"Azim's dynamic presentation, which fluidly involved the thoughts and ideas of the participants, touched our hearts with real-life examples of what true success means. Many who took part praised Azim's passion, sincerity and practical advice. We all valued the chance to sit and peacefully contemplate what was said, to focus on the important things in life and to gain insight into ourselves."

Helen Jordan, West Point Grey Academy Parent Representative

"As a public speaker myself, I understand that a speaker who is divinely inspired to see the perfection in their audience rather than one who is motivated by their own need to change the audience is a rare find. I am happy to report that you are such a speaker. All the participants found your presentation to be a 'life changing' experience. Your presence is proof that you are inspired by love. Thank you so much for being the best you that God has intended."

Angie Dairou, Co-ordinator, Breakfast with Soul

"Your ability to discuss the truly meaningful issues in life was much appreciated and much needed in our rushed and stressful lives. Feedback from participants included: 'Wonderful talk,' 'Much-needed presentation on the spiritual side of our lives,' 'I'm going to try to do things differently in my life.' It was a pleasure to meet you."

Pauline H. King, Program Manager,
Canada Customs & Revenue Agency

"We had an unprecedented number of people attend [Azim's seminar]... Azim's confident demeanor and calm presentation style was next to none. A high standard and great presentation."

Ann L. Pearson, Acting Health Promotion Manager,
BC Hydro, Canada

"Azim is a dynamic and a powerfully motivating speaker. He is excited and passionate about the things he talks about...very remarkable presentation."

Howard Greenstein, Executive Director, ACT II Child and Family Services keynote address at AGM in Vancouver, Canada

"I enjoyed your presentation and was very impressed with your positive attitude and energy. You energized and motivated me to read your book and put some of your insights into practice."

Kerry Jothen, CEO, Industry Training and Apprenticeship Commission (ITAC), British Columbia

"Dynamic, practical, and energizing presentation. The promotion of a balanced approach to business and life hit home and was really appreciated."

Participant at TD Bank Seminar for Entrepreneurs

"An excellent presenter, dynamic, stirring, passionate, concise and practical...."

Connie Larson, Burnaby Hospital Professional day address for palliative staff

"...relayed a lot of knowledge in a short time....excellent communicator, knows how to get the point across....thanks to Azim, I've finally learned how to take control of my life and destiny."

Nita Sharma, Amex; Fraseridge Realty on keynote presentation How to Make Your Vocation a Vacation

"Excellent presentation... good material, stories and thoughts... an excellent speaker!"

"Azim's presentations in Birmingham, Edinburgh, Leicester and London on 'Lifelong Learning —Key to Success' were inspiring, enlightening, thought-provoking and practical. The huge success of the event was clear from the large audiences that attended; they particularly enjoyed Azim's ability to engender audience participation."

"...Azim Jamal is a sought-after motivational speaker..."

For further details visit **www.azimjamal.com**
or e-mail: azim@azimjamal.com

To book Azim Jamal for your next event, contact:
Laura Fluter
Whitelight Promotions
whitelightpromo@telus.net
phone 604 929 7961

Order Form

Please send me:

	USA	Canada	Amount
____ Seven Steps to Lasting Happiness	$12.00	$16.00	____
____ Journal for Lasting Happiness	$15.00	$20.00	____
____ Seven Steps to Lasting Happiness (Audio CD)	$9.00	$12.00	____
____ The One-Minute Sufi	$12.00	$15.00	____
____ The Corporate Sufi	$12.00	$17.00	____
Plus General Sales Tax (7%)			____

Plus Shipping and Handling

	USA	Canada	
For first book or journal	$4.00	$4.00	____
Each additional book or journal	$3.00	$3.00	____
For CD	$2.00	$2.00	____
Total enclosed			____

Please turn over

Payment:

Please make check or money order payable to:
Azim Jamal, 10151 Gilmore Crescent, Richmond,
BC, V6X 1X1, Canada
E-mail: azim@azimjamal.com
Tel: 604-733-0737 Fax: 604-736-7511

For payment by credit card:

__ MasterCard __ Visa
Credit Card Account No.————————————————
Expiry Date ————————————————————————
Cardholder's Signature:————————————————

Ship to:

Name:————————————————————————
Address: (No PO Boxes please)————————————

City/State and Zip/Postal Code:————————————
Phone:————————————————————————

Thank you for your order